Second Annual National Conference on Science and the Law

Summary of Proceedings

San Diego, California
October 10–14, 2000

Sponsored by:
National Institute of Justice
American Bar Association, Criminal Justice Section
American Academy of Forensic Sciences
National Center for State Courts

In collaboration with:
National Academy of Sciences
Federal Judicial Center

May 2002
NCJ 191717

National Institute of Justice

Sarah V. Hart
Director

The National Institute of Justice is the research and development branch of the Department of Justice. NIJ's *Annual National Conference on Science and the Law* is part of its Professional Conference Series, which supports exchanges between researchers and practitioners through conferences, workshops, planning and development meetings, and other support to the criminal justice field.

The *Annual National Conference on Science and the Law* features speakers from the scientific, legal, and academic communities who are invited to speak on their fields. The conference was developed to foster dialogue among scientific and legal professionals and academics to promote further research.

The opinions expressed in this publication are those of the presenters and other persons attending the *Annual National Conference on Science and the Law*. They do not represent the official positions of the U.S. Department of Justice.

The National Institute of Justice is a component of the Office of Justice Programs, which also includes the Bureau of Justice Assistance, the Bureau of Justice Statistics, the Office of Juvenile Justice and Delinquency Prevention, and the Office for Victims of Crime.

Contents

Executive Summary v

Wednesday, October 11, 2000 1
    Welcoming Remarks 1
    Panel I. Training and Education 1
    Panel II. Cosponsor Information Session 3

Thursday, October 12, 2000 7
    Opening Remarks 7
    Keynote Address 7
    Panel III. Emerging Areas of Admissibility/Changing Standards of Admissibility 9
    Panel IV. Risk Assessment/Predictions of Dangerousness 11
    Panel V. Call-for-Papers Presentations 13
    Panel VI. Breakout Sessions 15

Friday, October 13, 2000 21
    Panel VII. What's Happening Now and May Happen in the Future With DNA
        Evidence 21
    Panel VIII. New Procedures for Identification 23
    Luncheon Presentation: Stalking—The Science, the Law, and Courtroom Dynamics 25
    Panel IX. Call-for-Papers Presentations 26
    Panel X. Breakout Sessions 28

Saturday, October 14, 2000 33
    Introduction to the Clutter Murder Case 33
    Panel XI. Blood and DNA Evidence 34
    Panel XII. Firearms and Toolmarks 36
    Panel XIII. Trace Evidence: Footprints 37
    Luncheon Presentation: The Truth May Be Out There—Forensic Science Meets the
        Television Industry 38
    Panel XIV. Trace Evidence: Rope and Tape 38
    Panel XV. Psychiatric and Psychological Evidence 39
    Panel XVI. Concluding Remarks 41

Executive Summary

The Second Annual National Conference on Science and the Law brought together members of the scientific, legal, and academic communities to examine and promote an understanding of science among legal professionals and to promote an understanding of the legal system among scientists.

The conference, held October 10–14, 2000, in San Diego, California, was sponsored by the National Institute of Justice, the American Bar Association, the American Academy of Forensic Sciences, and the National Center for State Courts in collaboration with the National Academy of Sciences and the Federal Judicial Center.

Conference speakers explored emerging areas and changing standards of admissibility; concerns surrounding risk assessment and predictions of dangerousness; expert testimony and the role of the judge, jurors, and attorneys; DNA evidence as it is used now and how it may be used in the future; and changes in the treatment of evidence admitted to the court, illustrated through discussions of the Clutter murder case of the 1960s. This report summarizes the conference presentations and discussions.

Education and Training in the Forensic Sciences

The opening day was marked by a discussion of the need for training and education in the forensic sciences. Panelists suggested that forensic scientists today need good education, skills training and testing, and training in ethics to meet the varied expectations of stakeholders such as investigators, instructing attorneys, and judges. Three necessary components for forensic science training and education were given:

- Education should occur in an institution that also conducts research, programs should be longer, and activities should reflect the skills students need in the field.
- Training should be outcome oriented, integrate new technology, and be applicable to specific real-world activities.
- Professional codes of ethics should regulate conduct, protect the public interest, be specific and honest in content, and be enforced.

Keynote Speaker Offers Comments on Opening Sessions

The keynote speaker, Duncan Moore of the White House Office of Science and Technology Policy, reaffirmed the value of enhancing cooperation among scientists, attorneys, and judges. He stressed the need to encourage cross-disciplinary efforts that fit science and technology into larger national goals and noted that science and technology are related to national economic growth issues. Dr. Moore challenged the audience to expand the scope of new partnerships for mutual benefit and suggested that such a move may encourage Congress to fund needed research and development. Dr. Moore closed by stating that continued and enhanced knowledge of the interaction between science and the law and the benefits of good technology do much to prevent crime and create a more just and crime-free society.

Admissibility Standards and Expert Testimony

During the second day, panelists discussed emerging areas and changing standards of admissibility. They pointed out that judges and juries must make decisions on techniques with which they are not familiar. The *Frye* test, which demonstrates general acceptance of a novel scientific technique, had been the state of the law everywhere. The *Daubert* ruling changed the emphasis to reliability rather than general acceptance. With the *Daubert* ruling, trial judges have had to determine whether expert testimony is reliable enough to be admitted into evidence. In an attempt to provide more guidance to courts, these two landmark cases on rules of evidence have been further scrutinized under New Rule 702 as it relates to the reliability of a scientific method or principle. In view of these changing standards, participants held that judges, experts, and lawyers must work together to maintain effective courtrooms and protect the constitutional rights of defendants.

Risk Assessment and Predictions of Dangerousness

Panelists discussed expert testimony that assesses risk and predicts dangerousness in mentally disordered offenders and sex offenders. Risk assessment represents a real concern because predicting dangerousness is particularly important in determining sentences. Panelists expressed a need for research to move from an almost exclusive focus on the individual when examining connections between mental health and criminal and violent behavior. They recommended that environmental and contextual contributors be considered as well. The discussants stressed that although some risk factors may correlate with future violence, they do not necessarily predict violent crime, and predictors, correlates, and causes found in one group may not apply to other groups. For example, predictors, correlates, and causes in sex offenders may not apply to violent offenders who have committed nonsexual crimes.

Law and psychiatry professor Mr. Christopher Slobogin stated that in making sentencing judgments, the predictive values of instruments alone are not yet clear and convincing enough. Estimates of 40-, 50-, or 60-percent likelihood cannot satisfy *beyond a reasonable doubt*. Predicting a repeat of violent behaviors must take into consideration a combination of prior convictions, clinical diagnoses, and predictive instruments. And, under admissibility standards such as *Frye,* consideration must be given not only to the instrument's validity but also to whether its use adds to or subtracts from the decision process.

DNA Evidence Now and for the Future

A central issue in the discussion—the current and future use of DNA—has stimulated considerable political and ethical debate that revolves around the access to and use of genetic testing to predict criminal behavior. Some States allow access to DNA databanks by law enforcement for improvement of the criminal justice system. The panel discussion on genetic evidence covered a range of issues, including its use in violence prevention and its impact on trial outcomes. Using genetic evidence to prevent violence, however, departs from the constitutional understanding that individuals cannot be condemned for *potential* dangerousness. Panelists asserted that if violence were to be medicalized to this extent, a person who has specific genetic markers might be detained or given drug therapy as a type of preventive "quarantine." The constitutional framework is shifting, however, as many States consider legislation to give convicted persons the right to DNA testing on evidence that had not been made available previously.

Renegotiations of Science

The "renegotiations" of science—conflicting views of what does and does not constitute truly scientific knowledge—were discussed extensively in panel sessions. One view holds that "truly scientific" evidence should provide greater certainty than "ordinary" evidence. The use of fingerprinting in connection with investigations was used to illustrate the renegotiations. Fingerprint matches have historically been framed to the courts as facts; it is widely accepted that no two people have the same fingerprints, which confirms unique identification. The *Daubert* court, however, stated that in science there are no certainties, only probabilistic results. As a result, scrutiny of forensic evidence, including fingerprinting, came under fire because the same finger will not produce exactly the same fingerprint twice in a row, and the impression from a small area of a fingerprint may, in fact, match any number of different fingers. Discussants noted how this example of the *reconstruction* of science illustrates the active roles that law and science play in the criminal justice system.

Evolving Treatment of Evidence

The conference ended with a lengthy discussion of the Clutter murder case, which served as an example of how the treatment and admissibility of evidence has changed in the years since the case came to trial. Physical evidence from the case, such as footprints, cut telephone cords, a shotgun, and bloodstained boots, illustrated that while the science behind the scrutiny of some evidence (e.g., blood) has undergone a paradigm shift, the science behind other evidence (e.g., tape) has changed little. Other case evidence, such as psychiatric and psychological profiles and an individual's competency to stand trial, has undergone significant change in the intervening years. In 1959, however, no tools were available to evaluate such competence, and no record exists of what the commission doctors for the case actually did with the two defendants. At the time of the Clutter case, mental health defenses were in their infancy and psychiatrists were not used. The prevailing fear then was that offenders would be released improperly, thus portraying a justice system that lacked in accountability and therefore was vulnerable to political ridicule.

Evolving Treatment of Evidence

Discussants concluded the retrospective analysis of the Clutter case by noting areas in which decisions made at the time would be unlikely to occur in a court today. For example, it is now unlikely that a jury would be composed only of men; a defendant's head injury would not be entered into record; opposition to capital punishment would not be a criterion for rejection from serving on a jury; and under *habeas corpus*, a confession incriminating another defendant could be entered into the record.

Participants also suggested that, had the defendants received better representation, they would likely have received a retrial. A district attorney concluded the discussion by stating that, given the retrospective analysis of the Clutter case evidence, he did not believe he would have pursued the death penalty.

Wednesday, October 11, 2000

Welcoming Remarks

David G. Boyd, Director, Office of Science and Technology (OS&T), National Institute of Justice (NIJ), welcomed conference attendees and described some of NIJ's activities and goals to improve the understanding between scientists and attorneys. Recent research funded by NIJ has addressed cross-jurisdictional communications—wireless interoperability, standards for and testing of police equipment such as DNA test kits, nonintrusive identification of hidden weapons, and development of paint databases for crimes involving cars. Past funded research has included postmortem identification through the study of insects. NIJ also investigates the legitimacy of equipment marketed as useful to local police organizations.

Dr. Boyd raised several questions: How should scientific and technological techniques, especially new ones, best be explained to juries and courts? How should a solid scientific foundation for the law be developed? Can science be used to strengthen evidence in advance of trial? Dr. Boyd invited practitioners to actively participate and encouraged them to ask the "hard questions."

Panel I. Training and Education

Carole Chaski, executive director, Institute for Linguistic Evidence, Georgetown, Delaware, introduced and moderated the panel on education and training for forensic scientists. She said that forensic science often has borrowed methodologies and problem-solving techniques from police crime laboratories. Technologists frequently receive practical training rather than classroom study in the theories behind forensic science. She framed the discussion by asking what efforts should be made to bridge these backgrounds and give scientific evidence a firmer basis in court.

Robert E. Gaensslen, professor and director of graduate studies, Forensic Science Program, University of Illinois at Chicago (UIC), discussed the forensic science residency. Part of the educational process, he explained, is to transmit core values in and the roles of research. Ethics should be an integral part of the curriculum in forensic science. The 2-year residency program helps develop the high skill level needed in practice. It could be considered similar to the third or fourth year in the clinical medical/dental model in which students usually participate in more hands-on training.

Criminalistics includes all the work that normally happens in a crime lab. Most forensic specialists in crime laboratories have a B.S. in chemistry or biology; some have a Ph.D. in molecular biology. Criminalistics as a profession has peculiarities. Criminalists, said Dr. Gaensslen, explain evidence and information to lay people. UIC's program represents an add-on rather than a substitute for hands-on training. The program—a partnership with the Illinois State Police, which has a renowned training program—provides university students with practical field experience and case work. Candidates for the program are carefully screened through interviews, background checks, and polygraphs.

Kim Herd, senior attorney and program manager, DNA Legal Assistance Unit, American Prosecutors Research Institute (APRI), Alexandria, Virginia, spoke about technical assistance and training on the use of DNA evidence that APRI offers to prosecutors. APRI also has programs on forensic science issues pertaining to drug-facilitated rapes and the use of dental records in investigations. The work of the DNA Legal Assistance Unit, said Ms. Herd, includes case law summarization on DNA evidence, help in developing "cold hit" units, resolution of databank issues (e.g., sampling and typing, change of techniques), admissibility of STR (short tandem repeat) technology, and extending statutes of limitations for rape cases. Attorneys' understanding of statistics and how they relate to the evidence they present often is weak. APRI has been conducting intensive regional training programs and programs in individual States.

Several advisory groups meet at APRI. Distinguished professors participate in the training for judges and contribute material. Students' comments are considered in course designs on such topics as background science for and forensic use of DNA polymarker methods (RFLP [restriction fragment length polymorphism] and PCR [polymerase chain reaction]), evidence collection and preservation, use of codes, and advanced background science. This training, however, reaches only a few of the thousands of prosecutors. Additional funding is needed to help educate more attorneys to use specialized evidence fairly and effectively.

William Tilstone, executive director, National Forensic Science Technology Center, Largo, Florida, acknowledged the influence of his earlier experience as a professor teaching master's-level forensic sciences at the University of Strathclyde (Glasgow, Scotland) and as director of the state crime laboratories in South Australia. Practically speaking, he said, academics do not know enough. Forensic scientists today need good education, skills training and testing, and training in ethics to be able to meet stakeholder expectations in a professional manner. Tilstone asked the participants to consider how broad stakeholder groups could be: immediate users such as investigators and instructing attorneys; secondary users such as judges, defenders, and determiners of fact; scientists conducting peer reviews; funders of research; and the public at large. Assessment is the key to achieving these needs; it can define required performance, measure actual performance, involve outside beneficial groups, and continue an ongoing measurement system. He noted the following necessary aspects:

- *Education* should be learning oriented in an institution that also conducts research; programs should be longer with examinations and transportable qualifications.
- *Training* often can be delivered at the workplace and should be outcome oriented. It must always be available to integrate new technology and should be situation specific, especially regarding DNA.
- *Professional codes of ethics*, the guiding beliefs that define a group, should regulate conduct, protect the public interest, be specific and honest in content, and be enforceable and enforced (for example, see the code of ethics used by the American Society of Crime Laboratory Directors).

Assessments can give objective proof of training or education, relate to maintenance of professional certification (as is regularly required for attorneys and hairdressers), and be a basis for lifelong learning. Professional codes of ethics address procedures for resolving or avoiding conflict of interest as well as providing guidance for acceptable conduct in different situations. Assessments, standards development, training, and education priorities for forensic scientists will encourage the growth of professionalism. The occupation, said Dr. Tilstone, is growing away from a crafts-based service industry to a professional service. Certification and accreditation offer objective proofs to support this.

Victor Weedn, director of Biotechnology and Health Initiatives and principal research scientist, Carnegie Mellon University, Pittsburgh, Pennsylvania, emphasized using education as part of the conceptual framework for forensic sciences. Education imparts fundamental understanding of how to perform effective scientific analysis, how to troubleshoot problems, how to identify and answer relevant questions, and how to give courtroom testimony that will enlighten and persuade juries.

Dr. Weedn said the learned professions—historically the clergy, lawyers, and physicians—were linked to universities and research and were not connected to particular financial interests. For example, a prospective member of the clergy would be a college graduate who served an apprenticeship, was given an examination and ordained, and then was accepted by the congregation. Similar paths developed in the legal and medical fields.

Forensic scientists typically have a bachelor's degree and may have a master's degree in forensic science or American Board of Criminalistics certification. A person with an undergraduate degree in chemistry does not have a forensic science education and lacks the necessary laboratory disciplines, training in case synthesis, operational contexts, and professional networks. Dr. Weedn explained that the community of professors is important apart from its influence on students as a neutral body of credible expertise and as a source of literature for the field. Science in the academic sense—as a quest for truth, deep understanding, and experimental verification—has inherent credibility.

Forensic science represents a distinct discipline with specialized knowledge and context. Forensic testing deals with nonpristine specimens; trace levels are characteristic problems of the field. Computer science is a comparable discipline that at first was not well accepted in academia. The academic crisis in forensic sciences, said Dr. Weedn, results from a lack of infrastructure; aging faculty; and a professional community that is too small, often not laboratory based, and inadequately supported.

Panel II. Cosponsor Information Session

Moderator **Richard Rau**, senior program manager, Investigative and Forensic Sciences Division, Office of Science and Technology, NIJ, introduced presenters representing the organizations that sponsored the conference.

National Center for State Courts
Karen Gottlieb, formerly of the National Center for State Courts (NCSC), described the organization's divisions. The Research Division publishes court statistics. The Court Services Division conducts studies, such as its examination of gender bias in the courts for the State of Virginia. NCSC's International Programs Division and Office of Government Relations work in

developing countries on rule-of-law issues. In its Williamsburg, Virginia, headquarters, NCSC operates an educational technology center and the Court Technology Laboratory for the States.

One of NCSC's current efforts is its online discussion of DNA evidence (*http://www.ncsc.dni.us/ icm/distance/edforum.html*). In April 2000, NCSC conducted a course for State judges entitled "How to Tell Good Science from Bad Science." NCSC has built a secure Web site for State court judges—JudgeLink—that offers a place to share and discuss ideas on the admissibility of scientific evidence. This resource particularly benefits judges who are in remote parts of the United States. JudgeLink also is developing a capability to support offers of real-time advice.

Federal Judicial Center
Jennifer Evans Marsh, attorney and psychologist, Research Division, Federal Judicial Center (FJC), Washington, D.C., spoke about her organization's mission. FJC works to improve Federal court administration and conducts related research projects. Its researchers have developed a risk prediction index for Federal offenders under supervision that has been in use around the Nation for 6 years. FJC also has published a reference manual on scientific evidence that is posted on the Internet (*http://air.fjc.gov/public/fjcweb.nsf/pages/16*). It frequently conducts educational initiatives on the Federal Judiciary Television Network, its main forum for seminars. FJC also hosts national conferences; recent topics include national sentencing policy and border courts.

National Academies (National Research Council)
Anne-Marie Mazza, director, Science, Technology, and Law Program, The National Academies, Washington, D.C., said that the judiciary recently had asked the Academies to help resolve interdisciplinary concerns involving science, engineering, and the law. The Academies have started to implement several initiatives in this context. Her section is examining jury instructions pertaining to scientific subjects and is developing standards of ethics for court testimony, access to research data (e.g., those supporting decisions by the Environmental Protection Agency and the Food and Drug Administration), access to data sealed in litigation, and other similar issues.

American Academy of Forensic Sciences
John McDowell, president, American Academy of Forensic Sciences, and director, Oral Medicine and Forensic Sciences, School of Dentistry, University of Colorado, Denver, said that the American Academy of Forensic Sciences (AAFS) was established by pathologists in 1948. AAFS currently has more than 5,000 member scientists from 48 countries. AAFS offers continuing education in the forensic sciences and works with other countries, such as China, in forensic categories ranging from psychiatry to engineering to odontology. AAFS also has a jurisprudence section for lawyers.

American Bar Association
Thomas Smith, director, Criminal Justice Section, American Bar Association (ABA), Washington, D.C., said he joined the ABA about 20 years ago after working for a State legislature. He stressed that the ABA has strong credibility with Congress, executive agencies, and the courts. It has approximately 407,000 members and has associate memberships for non-lawyers.

The organization has recently published standards on electronic surveillance and has several initiatives relating to DNA. The ABA offers audiotaped information on DNA and continuing legal education on cyberspace crime, and it will be working on systematic checks to prevent wrongful convictions (a reference to the work of the Innocence Project).

National Institute of Justice

Anjali Swienton, senior forensic analyst, ACS Defense, Inc., a contractor with NIJ, described NIJ's offices and research missions. The Office of Research and Evaluation is concerned with social science and the human behavioral aspects of crime and justice. One example of its programs is Breaking the Cycle, directed toward innovative programming for drug-involved offenders. The Office of Development and Communications handles all NIJ publications.

NIJ works on technological issues such as interoperability of communications for law enforcement, crime mapping, and investigative and forensic sciences. NIJ has established technical working groups (TWGs) to advise the community on best recommended practices in these areas. These TWGs have published guides on many topics, including the National Commission on the Future of DNA Evidence, explosion and bombing scene investigation, death investigation, crime scene investigation, fire and arson scene investigation, and eyewitness evidence (*http://www.ojp.usdoj.gov/nij/pubs.htm*). In addition, NIJ funds research and work performed with the Combined DNA Index System (CODIS), a national database of DNA from convicted felons.

Question-and-Answer Session: Development of a Research Agenda

One participant asked the group to consider research to develop a probability-based tool for predicting the presence of certain types of evidence. This could be a decision-support instrument or system for police, with a "weighted screening scale." He said forensic evidence is becoming more important and too often is left at the scene by officers who do not have adequate training to identify and collect forensic evidence.

An attendee suggested that agencies should have multimedia training on crime scene investigation similar to that developed at the University of Vermont. The interactive technology is available, and the participant proposed that it should be on the Internet for general use. Ms. Swienton pointed out that each jurisdiction will have to format training of this type to suit its own requirements. She suggested that a "portal site" on the Internet, drawing on several agencies, could be developed. Guides, said Ms. Swienton, will be needed for agencies that are isolated, have a small staff, and do not own or have access to a computer.

A question was asked about science education for law students. Until the methods of teaching evidence are changed and included on bar exams, law schools will not consider the topic important. Essential courses, such as statistics and research design, should be taught in law schools. Dr. Mazza commented that the Academies are interested in more science education for the legal field. Mr. Smith, noting that the ABA works with accrediting law school curriculums, offered to communicate with persons who are familiar with curriculum requirements. **Paul Giannelli**, Albert J. Weatherhead III and Richard W. Weatherhead Professor of Law, Case Western Reserve University School of Law, Cleveland, Ohio, said only a few law schools have such courses, and they are not popular among students. Defense attorneys may be even more in need of this type of education, but no special funding exists to support it.

Thursday, October 12, 2000

Opening Remarks

Julie E. Samuels, Acting Director, NIJ, thanked the participants for sharing their time and expertise. She explained how NIJ's goals seek to protect the public and ensure justice. The Institute continues to pursue an agenda to improve the application of scientific evidence, including support for such research efforts as a guide for law enforcement on DNA evidence (available on CD-ROM), a guide on collecting and storing evidence, and a guide on eyewitness evidence (*http://www.ojp.usdoj.gov/nij/pubs.htm*). NIJ also has provided funding to States to improve and expand forensic services and laboratories and has given $15 million to help States reduce the backlog of DNA evidence awaiting analysis.

Clear understanding of the validity of evidence is critical; therefore, better communication and training for attorneys, judges, and jurors concerning scientific data are among NIJ's priorities. In particular, rural law enforcement and isolated courts do not have access to special investigation techniques for scientific evidence. They need help—something akin to a "practitioner toolbox"—to confront the complex practical and moral issues brought into the justice arena by advances in science. All of us, said Ms. Samuels, need to work together to build bridges between the scientific and criminal justice communities.

Through a video presentation, the U.S. Attorney General thanked the participants who have been contributing to technical working groups and the Commission on the Future of DNA Evidence. The Attorney General said this work is assisting the search for truth as never before. DNA's power to exonerate those wrongly convicted opens new technical arenas and poses significant issues for the system in terms of what should be admitted in court and what is constitutional. The criminal justice system now relies on DNA evidence to a large degree; but as databases grow and behavioral genetics and other scientific fields develop, consideration has to be given to what is right and ethical to protect the people.

DNA is not the only example. How should we deal, the Attorney General asked, with the "dark alleys of the information highway" and yet protect individual privacy? How should technology for concealed weapons detection be used, but with protocols that prevent profiling? How should advances in behavioral genetics be handled? The intersection of science and the law has grown more important as people rely on science to determine truth. Conference participants have the responsibility to wrestle with these questions and consider them proactively to avoid a wrong turn. The Attorney General commended the judges and scholars who are working together on these problems to seek to control technology rather than allow it to "control us."

Keynote Address

Duncan Moore, Associate Director for Technology, White House Office of Science and Technology Policy, Washington, D.C., congratulated NIJ, particularly for its role in enhancing cooperation among scientists, attorneys, and judges and identifying important issues for future research and dialogue. Encouraging cross-disciplinary efforts for national goals is not an easy task, he said, and the interagency working groups have become a new generation of vehicles for fitting science and technology into larger national missions.

Science and technology are economic growth issues. Dr. Moore pointed out that the National Institutes of Health usually gets a substantial budget because it connects science with everyone's health. Agencies that normally do not work together easily can increase available budgets by collaborating in key areas such as emerging nanotechnology. Nanotechnology allows materials to be built that are stronger and lighter than steel. For example, it may change the way that cars and planes are constructed. Dr. Moore explained how the Federal Government has a natural role in long-term research in such areas. More funds—about $18 billion in fiscal year 2001—are being made available to universities for peer-reviewed research. But forensics has benefited less than other scientific areas from this support.

In the political arena, said Dr. Moore, using simplified, targeted communication to package ideas for Congress is important. In the July 2000 meeting on crime technology, the White House group tried to "generate some grand challenges." Such challenges give those in Congress material on which they can focus. A valuable connection related to educational need is the lack of an adequate technology-educated workforce. The country will need many well-trained people in high technology fields. Although the number of Ph.D.s in the sciences has grown in the United States, few have been for engineering or computer science. Companies strongly rely on foreign graduates to fill these positions.

Another consideration, explained Dr. Moore, is the gap between public-sector and industry salaries, which is important as a general economic indicator. The cost of retaining technologically skilled staff is always lower than the cost of recruiting. The huge competition between the private and public sectors affects such issues as progress against cybercrime. Some government pay scales could be changed to retain technologically skilled workers.

Referring to the costs of crime to society, Dr. Moore said that new civil rights twists are arising with technological advances. Better cooperation among public agencies can assure that the right information goes to the right place. Dr. Moore also invited attendees to consider what may be known by 2010 about brain function and behavioral genetics. Are we in a position, he asked, to address the ethical questions?

Dr. Moore challenged the group to expand the scope of the new partnerships, difficult and "unnatural" as they may be. This will increase budgets possibly as much as 18 percent. The courts, he said, should be involved, but the U.S. Department of Education and the private sector, particularly laboratories, also can offer help for difficult cases. All sides of these partnerships can benefit, and the private sector may be able to "get the message to Congress" to fund needed research and development.

Enhanced education and training in science and the law—using scenario-based learning experiences and newer, more sophisticated tools for the criminal justice system—is extremely important. The legal community needs new opportunities and new curriculums in universities. This is not a question of making scientists out of lawyers or vice versa, but a matter of understanding implications in common language. Finally, Dr. Moore said, the public also has to be educated on the roles of science and the law. Scientific tools cannot "solve everything." They may even create less justice when applied incorrectly. We need, he stated, to understand the benefits of good technology that can help prevent crime and create a more just and crime-free society.

Panel III. Emerging Areas of Admissibility/Changing Standards of Admissibility

Kenneth Broun, Henry Brandis Professor of Law, University of North Carolina School of Law, Chapel Hill, recognizing that many participants were not trained in law, explained that an expert is permitted to give an opinion to the court only if the subject is helpful to the jury and if the expert is qualified to give the opinion. If it is not relevant and will not "advance the ball," the court will not allow the expert to present his or her opinion. Recently, problems have arisen because decisions are being made about techniques that are unfamiliar to most everyone. In the 1920s, a novel scientific technique could be used only if, as deemed in the *Frye* (*Frye* v. *United States*, 293 F. 1013 [D.C. Cir. 1923]) test, it had "gained general acceptance." *Frye* has been the subject of many cases, and demonstration of general acceptance used to be the state of the law everywhere.

However, both legal and definitional problems exist. In 1974, the Federal Rules of Evidence set criteria for expert testimony, but they did not mention general scientific acceptance or relevancy. The problem culminated with *Daubert* v. *Merrell Dow Pharmaceuticals, Inc.* (509 U.S. 579 [1993]). The Court placed the emphasis on reliability rather than on scientific acceptance. With this ruling, a trial judge has to determine whether the expert testimony is reliable enough to be admitted into evidence. Some questions typically connected to this are:

- Can the scientific technique be tested?
- Has it been subjected to peer review?
- Are there standards or controls?
- What is the rate of error involved?
- Has the expert extrapolated correctly?

Other cases have settled and agreed that the "gatekeeping decision" is within the discretion of the trial court judge, but contrasting schools of thought have developed regarding guidelines for the courts. Some believe the Federal Rules of Evidence should be left alone to allow developing case law to set standards; others favor amending the Rules.

The idea of reliability and the "fit to the case" are subject to differing interpretation. A recent opinion of Judge Weinstein in *Falise* v. *American Tobacco Company* (94 F. Supp. 2d 316 [E.D.N.Y. 2000]) approves of expert testimony for the most part but excludes certain aspects. The greatest threat is not the inclusion of "bad science" but, rather, that sound scientists would become discouraged with assessing the law. The good-faith attempt by *Daubert* to admit expert testimony, including that which is novel, is workable.

Leo Whinery, Alfred P. Murrah Professor, University of Oklahoma School of Law, Norman, referred the group to papers of the 1992 and 1995 drafting committees on the Federal Rules of

Evidence. Advances in the hard and soft sciences have created challenges to judges who fill a "gatekeeping" role on evidence. In 21 States, Mr. Whinery noted, the *Frye* rule is followed; 18 States have taken guidance from the *Daubert* rule; 8 States are "pre-*Daubert*," with varying reliability criteria; 5 States have uncertain admissibility standards; and 3 States have other admissibility standards. The dispute over Rule 702—"Testimony by Experts"—concerns the "probability of truth" that a method or principle is reliable. This accommodation involves some problematic interpretation: Is there a relevant scientific community? Does that community agree to accept this method or principle? The court nonetheless receives somewhat more guidance with Rule 702.

Edward Imwinkelried, professor, University of California, Davis, School of Law, asked what the starting point is for determining appropriate methodology. The trial judge's task is to decide if the appropriate methodology has been used. This requires a close look at the nature of the underlying claim:

- *Historical claim.* This is a simple claim that a practice or use exists in a field. For validity of a historical claim, collected *observation* is pivotal.
- *Credibility claim.* In this case, observation is not enough. For example, recanting or delayed reporting of a rape raises an issue of credibility for which *cumulative experience of a large number of clinicians* would indicate the required validity. The point would be not to prove whether or not a rape occurred but that someone who behaved that way could honestly believe she (or he) had been raped. Many women are treated on the basis of this criterion; though some may be lying, the large number of reports by experienced clinicians would indicate that the majority of the women are being truthful.
- *Substantive claim.* In this case, it is not merely a claim of connection or history but that this circumstance predicts another similar situation. The examiner needs a *validated database* of, for example, a large number of women treated for rape who exhibit certain symptoms such as those of posttraumatic stress disorder (PTSD). Meaningful validation has to be included, such as physical signs, police followup, confession evidence, and district attorney's (DA's) office convictions.

Myrna Raeder, professor, Southwestern University School of Law, Los Angeles, California, and past chairperson, Criminal Justice Section, ABA, spoke about the draft of the proposed amended version of Federal Rule of Evidence 702. This rule applies a three-pronged test: Is expert testimony based on sufficient facts or data? Are the data the product of reliable principles or methods? Has the expert witness applied the principles and methods reliably to the facts of the case? The amended rule, however, gives little guidance on procedures for judges, and its application involves some tough questions, particularly in terms of making experts available for indigent defendants and the discovery process.

One Florida study found that 83 percent of judges could not distinguish valid from flawed scientific evidence. One recommendation is to use technical advisors to the court. Duke University is building a databank of scientific advisors who could help judges understand complex scientific evidence. The neutrality of experts also comes under fire because of individual backgrounds and clientele. The judge is charged with controlling the courtroom, preventing confusion that does not help the task, and can, under Rule 403—"Exclusion of Relevant

Evidence on Grounds of Prejudice, Confusion, or Waste of Time"—exclude a witness if "sufficient prejudicial possibility outweighs the probative." In relation to the use of polygraphs, for example, cases have shown a varied and startling range of admissibility of test results and polygraphs often are excluded.

Ms. Raeder said careful thinking may be needed to keep certain "evidence" out. Judges, experts, and lawyers need to work together to set up an effective courtroom and protect the constitutional rights of defendants. She recommended the *Reference Manual on Scientific Evidence* (2d ed.), which is posted on the Web for judges and attorneys (*http://air.fjc.gov/public/fjcweb.nsf/pages/16*).

Question-and-Answer Session
A participant asked about statistical information on hair evidence relative to DNA exonerations. Are there discrepancies in expert testimony? What is the state of using eyewitness testimony? Ms. Raeder said there was concern about hair evidence. In the DNA exonerations, most cases involved mistaken identity, and some had used hair evidence. Cases that rely on hair evidence often are suspect because the datasets are small. Supreme Court cases have been argued on scientific reports of a "match" and what this means in terms of causation. *Daubert* arguments concern testability. At what point are you obliged to conduct major research, Ms. Raeder asked. Mr. Imwinkelried referred again to the underlying claim, and Mr. Broun suggested establishing guidelines but letting the courts work out specifics through case development.

Panel IV. Risk Assessment/Predictions of Dangerousness

Christopher Slobogin, Stephen C. O'Connell Professor of Law and affiliate professor of psychiatry, University of Florida Levin College of Law, Gainesville, introduced the session, explaining that risk assessment is a pervasive concern in the legal world. In criminal justice determinations, dangerousness is particularly important relative to sentencing. A mentally disordered offender who is considered dangerous will be incarcerated longer than one who is assessed as harmless. Expert testimony, therefore, is introduced on mentally disordered and sex offenders for assessing risk of repeat violent behavior.

Randy Otto, associate professor, Department of Mental Health Law & Policy, Florida Mental Health Institute, University of South Florida, Tampa, spoke about connections between mental health and violent behavior. Psychiatrists have a reputation for being more often wrong than right concerning the repetition of violent acts. In the past, efforts have focused on assessing the individual, but more research is needed on environmental and contextual contributors to this complicated topic. Some factors correlate with but do not necessarily predict the repeat of violent acts. When a study controls for co-variables on socioeconomic status, neighborhood, and employment, then factors that at first may appear related, such as ethnic minority, become unimportant. Predictors, correlates, and causes in one group may not apply to other groups; for example, predictors, correlates, and causes in sex offenders may not apply to violent offenders who have committed nonsexual crimes.

Advances have been made in conceptualizing violent behavior. In the newer construct, more focus is given to person-situation interaction and factors that will decrease or minimize risk. This is a probabilistic description.

Although the scientific community has made an unprecedented rush to accept actuarial approaches, the research does not validate the predictive power of unadjusted actuarials. Unstructured clinical assessment, on its own, has poor reliability and validity. Experience has shown that neither standard psychological testing nor unstructured clinical assessment has good predictive power. Statistically based actuarial assessments can be combined with clinical assessments and environmental factors. Items known to be related to violence risk are covered in such instruments as the competence assessment instrument and the sexual violence assessment. Substance use significantly increases the risk that the user will commit violence. For sexual offenders, 18 States have indeterminate civil commitment requirements. They use instruments with demonstrated levels of validity to identify risk and protective factors. Concerns about actuarial assessment arise particularly when the instrument is not used in the manner the authors suggested or is developed with one group of people but used on another.

Marnie Rice, director of research, Mental Health Centre, and professor of psychiatry and behavioural neurosciences, McMaster University, Penetanguishene, Ontario, spoke to the group about the Canadian followup database on sex offenders. In the 1980s, Monahan and associates showed that no more than one out of three predictions of violent behavior were accurate in predicting recidivism among sex offenders. Meehl and Monahan demonstrated that statistical prediction methods were better than unstructured assessments. Valuable ways have been devised to combine predictive tools; actuarial instruments can be adjusted for clinical perceptions.

In Canada, studies have been conducted on different predictive factors at a maximum security psychiatric institution. About 15 percent of the study group were sex offenders. The research looked at broadly ranged variables—demographic, childhood, psychiatric, criminal background—and "packaged" these to predict who would commit another offense. Steps were taken to use an instrument that could be cross-validated. Within 7 years, 31 percent of the population had committed a new offense (from common assault to murder). In the 1990s, the instrument was improved. It currently includes 12 variables and provides information comparable with the actual rate of recidivism among the sex offender population. Of people who scored above 0.8, 100 percent committed another offense.

Researchers have asked whether a "true sexual predator" exists. In studies of nonpsychopaths and deviant psychopaths, those who were nondeviant showed higher recidivism. In general, higher rates of violent recidivism are found among sex offenders; but the outcome measure has been debated. Should predictions look at new convictions for sexual offenses or violent offenses? Plea bargaining often affects the way offenses are recorded. Further, many sex offenders are not charged or convicted. In studies of sex offender laws, timeframes for the research also are unclear: Should the rest of an individual's life be considered, or only a specific time period?

In a new study of Canadian males using similar (albeit different) predictive instruments—referred to as "VRAG," or Violence Risk Appraisal Guide, and "SORAG," or Sexual Offender Risk Appraisal Guide—violent recidivism was predicted at 0.73, and strictly sexual recidivism was predicted at 0.65 to 0.66. This can be considered an adequate prediction of reoffense. Many articles have been published on these studies and on cross-studies of mentally disordered, institutionalized, and sex-offending persons. These methods can be seen as meeting the *Daubert* criteria—whether a technique has been tested, subjected to peer review, and published as reliable. Some of these assessments are strong enough to use in a courtroom.

Mr. Slobogin noted that, for the law, prediction may not be good enough. "Clear and convincing" or "beyond a reasonable doubt" cannot be satisfied with a 40-, 50-, or even 60-percent likelihood. Prior convictions, clinical diagnoses, and predictive instruments will have to be considered in combination. Under the *Frye* rule, clinical predictions are routinely accepted, especially for civil commitments, even though they are acknowledged as being "not very good." Many of the newer instruments, however, are rejected under *Frye*. The factfinder has to consider not only whether the instrument has validity but whether it adds to or subtracts from the decision process.

Question-and-Answer Session
An attendee commented that most judges do not understand the meaning of correlation; it is not particularly useful until a "0.9" case comes before the court. Dr. Rice said the Violence Risk Appraisal Guide uses a "confidence score" over a period of time—the idea of incremental validity. In the case of the polygraph, the courts have kept out testimony because of the known error rates. As actuarial instruments improve, a higher "comfort level" can be reached.

An audience member asked about the effect on risk assessment of particular treatment efforts for sex offending or the lapse of time, such as a period of 7 years. Panel members agreed that no currently known treatment would affect the risk assessment.

Mr. Slobogin described a MacArthur Foundation project that is integrating an actuarial flow chart into a prediction tree. Counsel has to weigh the prejudicial influence this might have on a jury. John Monahan, the grandfather of prediction research, studied how phrasing a question differently for identical information could affect the response, which is an important evidentiary issue.

Panel V. Call-for-Papers Presentations

An Analysis of the Impact of Juror Characteristics and Contextual Factors on Appraisal of Expert Testimony
Stephen Golding, professor, Department of Psychology, University of Utah, Salt Lake City, presented his paper on decisional reliability and juror qualities. Criminal justice decisions that vary widely and are unreliable, said Dr. Golding, are not just. Adjudication leading to radically different outcomes appears capricious and will not be tolerated. Evidence should be constructed and presented so as to produce the best possible accuracy and reliability, which requires being mindful of procedural rules and the jury's role as trier of fact.

Systemwide factors contribute to decisional reliability. The failure to attend to a varying cadre of experts (for example, specialize in different fields, hold differing views, receive various levels of training, and whose reputations are either well or poorly regarded) and an inaccurate tendency to view jurors as "blank slates," Dr. Golding explained, has affected this reliability. The rituals of the legal process, such as *voir dire*, which begin well before trial, affect jurors' views of their roles and their interpretation of the evidence. Why is it that poorly qualified experts are more common among trial experts than experts accredited for other purposes? Well-trained experts using state-of-the-art techniques, said Dr. Golding, would arrive at considerable agreement in most cases.

Jennifer Skeem, postdoctoral fellow in law and psychiatry, Western Psychiatric Institute and Clinic, University of Pittsburgh Medical Center, Pennsylvania, said that, according to research, jury-based trials demonstrate a lot of decisional unreliability because jurors' attitudes about the system, the crimes, and everyday events influence their verdicts more than judicial instructions do.

Good examples are in cases involving the insanity defense. Marked differences arise from personal conceptions of insanity. A study in Utah looked at the combination of features considered by a group of jurors to be "a prototype of insane behavior." Thirty percent of the features mentioned in responses were idiosyncratic. Respondents in the study would rate whether a particular feature was "essential to their concept of insanity." The severe mental disability framework, a prototype similar to the "wild beast test" of the 1700s, was chosen by 47 percent; 33 percent selected the "moral insanity" version, which conflates psychopathy and psychosis with a detached and unpredictably violent offender, popular in media portrayals; and 21 percent took the mental-state-centered (MSC) view that a person was impaired in a mental state relatively exclusively at the time of offense.

How does this affect verdicts? In a case at law, Dr. Skeem explained, the person deemed to have MSC characteristics is more likely to be found "not guilty due to insanity" than the other two groups. The verdict will depend on the composition and preconceptions of the jury.

*Views From the Bench: Judges on Judging Scientific Evidence Post-*Daubert

James Richardson, director, Master of Judicial Studies Program, and professor of sociology and judicial studies, University of Nevada, Reno, described a study of trial judges, who are the "gatekeepers" for evidence. Of the 400 judges studied, 50 percent had been on the bench for 10 years, 31 percent for 5 to 10 years, and 19 percent less than 5 years. The judges were given a choice of a mail-out questionnaire or telephone survey (i.e., a structured interview). For part one, 71 percent responded; for part two, 81 percent responded. The study, conducted by the University of Nevada, Reno, and funded in part by the Federal Judicial Center, was completed prior to the *Kumho Tire Co. Ltd.* v. *Carmichael* (526 U.S. 137 [1999]) decision.

More than half the group—55 percent—found the *Daubert* decision to have great value, 39 percent said it had "some value," and 6 percent thought it had "no value." Nearly all the judges (91 percent) believed the judicial gatekeeping function toward evidence was appropriate. Those who said it was inappropriate stated they were not prepared enough to make that decision. The concepts of peer review and general acceptance were well understood, while falsifiability and error-rate comparisons were not well understood.

The questionnaire inquired into the judges' perceptions of the utility of the falsifiability criteria. More than 90 percent said the decision was very or somewhat useful, but almost 60 percent said they did not understand the concept well. Of the 88 percent who said the concept of falsifiability was useful, only 6 percent had a "true understanding" of what it meant. The group was asked which specific guideline was most important. General acceptance was chosen by 51 percent, falsifiability by 18 percent, error rates by 16 percent, and peer-reviewed study by 14 percent.

In distinguishing science from technical or specialized knowledge, most judges said the "fit to the case" was more important than defining whether the evidence was "science" or "technical method." Approximately 84 percent thought survey research was not scientific. Clinical psychological assessment was considered scientific by 60 percent, while 56 percent said engineering was scientific. Most said that technical or specialized knowledge was not clearly distinguished. They said they found scientific evidence useful, but the extent of their understanding and ability to apply it well "was questionable."

The study has implications for new technological developments. Judges have broad latitude to admit all forms of expert testimony and do not differentiate between scientific and technical evidence. The judges expressed a desire for more overview of the philosophy and methods of science, but not on philosophy or methods of law. Dr. Sophia Gatowski, panelist, referred the audience to *A Judge's Deskbook on the Basic Philosophies and Methods of Science: Model Curriculum* (posted on the Web at *http://www.unr.edu/bench*).

Panel VI. Breakout Sessions

Practical and Ethical Dilemmas Confronting Testifying Experts—Where Attorneys' Questions Go Wrong

Susan Fisch, deputy State public defender, trial office training director, Colorado State Office of the Public Defender, Denver, stressed the importance of preparing before trial all experts an attorney intends to put on the witness stand. Preparation includes reviewing all material asked for on discovery, any results and/or opinions to which the expert will testify, and potential areas of weakness that may be targeted on cross-examination. Ms. Fisch also emphasized the importance of ensuring that when the expert is a scientist or other non-legal specialist, the attorney clearly explains the legal language that will be used in questioning and presenting evidence.

As an expert, it is important to demand that the presenting attorney explain what he or she expects of the testimony. When the opposing side presents an expert, the other attorney must investigate the expert's background, avoid stipulating to his or her qualifications, and ask questions on *voir dire* that may weaken the expert's credibility. The attorney needs to research the area of expertise that will be presented, even if it means hiring an expert of his or her own as an advisor so that truly meaningful questions can be asked and the most helpful answers can be elicited.

Experts, explained Ms. Fisch, are supposed to be nonpartisan; because of this, no legal requirements prohibit experts from speaking with opposing attorneys prior to trial. In light of this, an attorney should always ask for a meeting with opposing experts. If denied, he or she can send a letter noting for the record that the request was denied and introduce the letter before the court when the expert is on the witness stand to show potential bias. Other ways to attack damaging expert testimony are to obtain transcripts of the expert's past testimony or depositions that he or she may have testified contrary to the instant case, all standard operating procedures relied on by the expert in testing to determine whether he or she followed those procedures in the instant case, and indications of fee arrangements (if any) with the presenting side.

Paul Giannelli, Case Western Reserve University School of Law, Cleveland, Ohio, stated that it was the government's responsibility to deal fairly with scientific evidence, especially when the court provides counsel for indigent defendants. He suggested that to litigate competently in the current tenor of the criminal courts, an attorney must have some grounding in science. Few law schools, however, adequately prepare their students to deal with scientific testimony. Although scientific experts can be quite useful to a trier of fact, the attorneys who offer the witnesses are responsible for them. An attorney is responsible for ensuring that the expert possesses the credentials he or she claims, is not overstating conclusions drawn from less-than-conclusive results, and is clarifying—rather than hopelessly convoluting—the issues at hand. Mr. Giannelli gave several examples of actual cases in which conclusions were misrepresented, reports intentionally had been worded so as to mislead, and experts were pressured by presenting attorneys to give testimony that went against their professional ethics. In addition, Mr. Giannelli passed out a 20-page handout with numerous examples of cases in which an attorney, an expert, or both behaved unethically in the manner of presentation or interpretation of scientific evidence.

Evaluating Psychological Syndrome Testimony: Admissibility Challenges Under Frye *and* Daubert/Joiner/Kumho

Carole Chaski, moderator of the session, introduced **Margaret A. Hagen**, professor, Department of Psychology, Boston University, Massachusetts, who has worked on visual perception and legal aspects of psychology. Dr. Hagen asked the following questions concerning debates about the definition of science: Is it a monolithic body of knowledge? Is it theorem proving? Is it problem solving? Lawyers may think of science as a monolithic body of knowledge, she said, while scientists think more about collecting data and proving or disproving ideas. American law is exercised in an adversarial system, and two or three interpretations of data always are presented. In science, positions differ, considerations of what counts as data vary, valid collection methods abound, and interpretation techniques vary. Working through these to a particular conclusion is a dialectic.

Definitions for "syndrome" vary. Dr. Hagen considered three particular ones: child sexual abuse (CSA) accommodation syndrome, rape trauma (RT) syndrome, and battered woman (BW) syndrome. She said clinical observations are subjective and vary according to training, experience, and education. In these syndromes, she continued, no evidence exists that variables can discriminate whether the abuse took place, no clear pattern is discerned, and no common definitions or symptoms are tested with a controlled scientific experiment. The syndromes cannot be said to "in fact exist."

RT, Dr. Hagen explained, was driven by feminist thought in the 1970s and first discussed in connection with an interview study of only 13 women. Sampling, controls, and measuring devices were not used. RT simply is invoked as an explanation why some women do not report rape. BW has been described as showing accumulated terror and perception of danger, "learned helplessness," and failure to attempt to escape from the abuser. Interviews, however, have failed to record time periods, and no definite cyclical patterns has been established. Documentation of accumulated terror, which is important to courts, and the possibility of testing the escalation to violence are not included. BW simply is a popular explanation why some women do not escape when they could. Dr. Hagen noted that connections between symptoms and a supposed "triggering event" often are questionable. In addition, blind tests of the hypotheses or independent corroboration of claims are not demonstrated across clinicians, patients, or separate research efforts.

Testability or falsifiability depends on accurate measurement. If definitions are not clear and consistent, then measurements cannot be performed. Research on error rates for syndrome diagnoses across clinics or individual professionals have not been published. In scientific research, instrument bias is considered a crucial factor; it might be explained as the effect of expectation on the outcome of a study. In syndrome methodology, "measurement" is subject to a great deal of bias and placebo effects. Dr. Hagen concluded that syndrome research could not be considered science under *Daubert* criteria. It lacks scientific support in peer-reviewed journals and general acceptance in the scientific community.

Lenore Walker, professor of psychology, Center for Psychological Studies, Nova Southeastern University, Ft. Lauderdale, Florida, said she would agree that there are many examples of poor science in the psychological arena. In the cases of battered women, though, systematic collection of data and observable factors occurring in a pattern can be found. The syndrome is used to explain counterintuitive events in legal conflicts and to answer questions about "state of mind" in a legal context. Not all syndromes are psychiatric diagnoses, and it would be incorrect to consider them as mental illnesses. The syndrome definition can help answer difficult questions in particular contexts. Many such syndromes have been found useful: PTSD, BW, CSA, parental alienation, premenstrual syndrome, and urban stress are examples. Demanding strict scientific critiques of methodology leaves the courts with no guidance.

In the example of PTSD, Ms. Walker elaborated, characteristic categories include intrusive recollections, arousal (anxiety), and avoidance symptoms (depression, repression). Although some theoretical explanations such as "learned helplessness" may be connected to a syndrome such as BW, these are not necessarily part of the syndrome. The dynamics of abuse are not the same as symptoms of a disease. Placebo effects occur.

By combining the differing approaches of scientific inductive methods and reasoning or deductive methods, the truth may come out. In science, the examiner analyzes variables for causal and *other* relationships, using, for example, randomly assigned experimental groups, standardized tests, historical self-reports, pretests and posttests, and clinical inference. Standards after *Daubert* and *Kumho* have been continually reinterpreted. Statistical analysis can help guide the court by manipulating variables and making clear a "known error rate" or falsifiability of impressions created by the data. In law, the examiner is not allowed to "start with the answer." For psychological phenomena, different standards of significance exist that may apply under the law. "Beyond reasonable doubt" might be considered as 99 percent certain, while "clear and convincing" could mean about 75 percent, and "more likely than not" would be only 51 percent.

The American Psychological Association (APA) is monitoring mental health courts to examine the value of getting persons with mental problems out of the criminal justice system at the point of arrest. Many potential areas between the mental health system and criminal justice system exist. Out of 40 women in Dr. Walker's battered women study, 39 were also abuse survivors, and many were drug involved. Researchers have to ask what makes a good clinical opinion. This must be done carefully and based on more than one test. A diagnosis of "parental alienation syndrome" may not be distinguishable from other problems, but courts are intuitively admitting it for consideration. APA has published a report on violence in the family. Battered women's syndrome forms a pattern in the context of intimate relationships. Juries and judges must evaluate clinical material and patterns to separate these from "junk science."

Syndrome terminology, Dr. Walker explained, can be considered "shortcuts" that refer to known patterns in psychological assessments. However, for the sake of attorneys who must explain cases to juries and judges, certain wording has to be clearly defined. In New York law, for example, "delayed outcry" and "failure to leave" have specific implications. One conference participant pointed out that prosecutors rarely meet with victims. If the victim has not been examined, testimony can be presented only on "common characteristics." That information will look quite different depending on who presents it to the court. Another person in the audience asked about clearly distinguishing overuse or misuse of syndrome evidence. Dr. Walker responded that it is critical to use a two-stage approach to psychological evidence: first, evaluate it and give it to the attorneys; second, decide what should be used.

The Use of Forensic Entomology in Postmortem Interval Determinations

Jason Byrd, forensic entomologist and assistant professor of criminal justice, Department of Biology and Department of Criminal Justice, Virginia Commonwealth University, Richmond, and **Neal Haskell**, firearms and forensic entomology consultant, Rensselaer, Indiana, spoke to the group on the applications of this science. Entomology—the study of insects—is being increasingly used in forensic investigations. The science of forensic entomology is used in several contexts: urban, stored product, and medicocriminal/medicolegal. In the urban context, entomological investigation is used to support civil litigation, for example, in cases of termite infestation. In the stored product context, food contamination is investigated to determine where the infestation occurred and whether it was intentional or accidental. In the medicocriminal/medicolegal arena—the focus of this session—forensic entomology is used to determine the succession of insects and their arthropod relatives on a human cadaver, which can be analyzed to determine the postmortem interval (or time since death), and other facts surrounding the death (e.g., location, placement or movement of the body, manner of death).

Entomological evidence, explained Byrd and Haskell, has been widely accepted as scientific evidence in the courts. A homicide case in Oklahoma demonstrated the value of entomological evidence in both the investigation and pretrial stages. The defendant's claim as to when she last saw her deceased husband was disproved by the third-stage maggot accumulation on his body; she eventually was convicted of murdering him. In the analysis were critical climatological data, the time delay from death until colonization, the effect of the maggot mass temperature on development, and the nocturnal absence of blow flies.

Because insects can be present on a cadaver for up to 2½ years, delays that often occur in recovering remains, as in missing persons cases, do not preclude the collection and use of entomological evidence to aid investigations. Forensic entomology also provides answers in even older cases. Because insects will feed first on the soft-tissue areas of the head, such as the eyes and nasal passages, and any open wounds, they often will neglect areas of undamaged flesh that will be left intact to harden. Many years after death, human remains can be found and, through entomological analysis, give useful information concerning the cause and manner of death as well as the approximate time of death.

Trace Evidence: The Smallest Things Can Make the Biggest Difference
Elizabeth Farris, chief trial counsel, Hampden County DA's Office, Springfield, Massachusetts, spoke about the legal implications of using trace evidence at trial. She discussed the possible ramifications of investigators' failure to recognize and/or collect potentially probative evidence. Ms. Farris explained the difference between failure to collect and "lost" evidence—that which is collected from the crime scene but is never analyzed or goes missing before trial. She discussed the standards of admissibility for new and established sciences under *Daubert, General Electric Co.* v. *Joiner* (522 U.S. 136 [1997]) and *Kumho Tire Co. Ltd.* v. *Carmichael*.

Under the *Brady* rule (*Brady* v. *Maryland*, 373 U.S. 83 [1963]), the State is required to turn over any and all exculpatory evidence to the defense. In most States, "missing" evidence or failure to turn over evidence violates *Brady* only if it is found to have been done in bad faith, it was known that the evidence was exculpatory, and it was intentionally withheld. Potentially useful but not conclusively exculpatory information does not necessarily need to be turned over. To prevail on a *Brady* claim, the defendant must prove official animus or a conscious effort to suppress exculpatory evidence.

Ms. Farris presented a case study in which trace evidence, including blood, fibers, and paint, was pivotal to solving the case. Through crime scene photographs, certain items of evidence were introduced at trial, although the original items were claimed "lost" by the crime lab. The prosecutor was able to secure a conviction with only the photographs. Upon retrial, the "lost" evidence was located and tested. Lab results confirmed what prosecutors had suspected, and the conviction was affirmed.

Marjorie Harris, senior forensic scientist, Division of Forensic Science, Commonwealth of Virginia, Richmond, discussed trace evidence from a scientist's perspective. She discussed a high-profile case that occurred in Virginia in 1989 in which a 5-year-old girl disappeared from a Christmas party. Following witness tips, police apprehended a maintenance man who worked in the building where the girl lived. When he was found, he was washing his clothes, including a jacket and shoes, and a sheath from a knife. When charged with the abduction, he never denied it; he only challenged the police to prove it. Scientists collected evidence from the suspect's car, including tape lifts from the car seats. The girl's body was never recovered; to this day it has not been found. For comparison purposes, investigators tracked down the outfit she had been wearing when she disappeared. Only a limited number had been made and sold through J.C. Penney's catalogue. After seeing a flier about the outfit, a man in Kentucky who had bought the same outfit for his granddaughter donated the garment to the investigation. Several blue acrylic fibers were recovered from the suspect's car that were consistent with the make of outfit the girl had been wearing. In addition, fibers were discovered that matched a black dyed rabbit-hair coat the girl's mother had been wearing the night of the abduction.

The three main motives for abducting a child are to gain custody (when it is a noncustodial parent), ask for ransom, and defile. The suspect was not related to the girl, and no ransom note was received. He was charged with abduction with intent to defile. The case hinged largely on the trace evidence. Though the suspect never confessed and the body was never found, he was convicted and sentenced to 50 years.

Friday, October 13, 2000

Panel VII. What's Happening Now and May Happen in the Future With DNA Evidence

Deborah Denno, professor, Fordham University School of Law, New York, New York, discussed recent developments in behavioral genetics from the point of view of the law. The idea that biological factors may contribute to criminal behavior has been given wide acceptance among scientists and criminologists, but it has been resisted in court on the rare occasions when the defense has attempted to use it. Research on genetic predictors of criminal behavior has stimulated much political and ethical debate.

In the murder case against Steven Mobley in Georgia (*Mobley* v. *State of Georgia*, 455 S.E. 2d 61 Ga. 1995), defense attorneys found little in his wealthy background that could be sympathetic to a jury. During family interviews, they uncovered four generations of "bad people," individuals who, although successful in business, had descriptions as being "deranged and aggressive." Spurred by this information and a study from the Netherlands about a family that showed genetic MAOA (monoamine oxidase A) deficiency—believed to have afflicted several generations of the men in that family with retardation and bizarre sexual behavior—Mobley's attorneys applied to have him tested genetically. The court denied the request. It claimed that too little scientific evidence existed to allow the testing and would not admit test information as a mitigating factor. Why, asked Dr. Denno, has this kind of evidence been shunned by the courts?

One aspect, she said, is that genetic evidence has the appearance of great precision, an "aura" that could have too much impact on a jury, regardless of the politics. It also "cuts both ways" and might hurt rather than help a defendant. Any geneticist would agree that a strong interaction exists between what the genes pass on and the environment. It is a myth that this could "mark people." The third and strongest reason for legal resistance are moral and ethical concerns that go back to the concept of free will and the time of Nazi genetic experimentation. No evidence exists, said Dr. Denno, on whether we have free will or not. Much concern is expressed, however, about the possible stigmatizing effect of such information and the need to preserve social responsibility. If genetic evidence is so controversial, she asked, why can we not simply say it is too morally and ethically problematic rather than calling it "bad science?"

Lori Andrews, professor and director, Institute for Science, Law and Technology, Illinois Institute of Technology, Chicago-Kent College of Law, served as chairperson of the Federal Working Group on the Ethical, Legal, and Social Implications of the Human Genome Project and heard such claims as "the nature/nurture debate is all over—it is all nature," and "soon we will find the genes for violence." In a study of genetic counselors, a substantial number said they would favor the abortion of a fetus with such violence-connected genes, although a study of people with such genetic limitations has not been conducted to determine if they are law abiding.

People who could take part in such a study, Ms. Andrews said, could easily be identified, possibly among prisoners. Even beyond the forensic DNA databank, hospitals today already take sample DNA and screen newborns on an ongoing basis. The U.S. Department of Defense collects DNA information on all members of the military.

In State definitions of allowable access to DNA databanks, access often is permitted for "law enforcement or improvement of the criminal justice system." Some forensic DNA databanks require samples from misdemeanants or arrestees. Law enforcement already has accessed newborn screening databanks in some circumstances. Privacy concerns have been voiced by the American Civil Liberties Union, but courts will probably ignore them. Should the fourth amendment to the Constitution, asked Ms. Andrews, apply to secondary uses of DNA samples?

Additional research on the XYY genetic syndrome—when a male has two Y chromosomes—has seemed precise and fear producing. A study of 8,600 children in Chicago was conducted as part of a National Institutes of Health (NIH) violence prevention program. Part of the study showed that children who were aggressive in school were eight times more likely to commit crimes by age 30.

In the health setting, Ms. Andrews continued, NIH is looking at low levels of serotonin and violent behavior as well as the possibilities of using gene therapy to "repair" a genetic deficiency. Social intervention may not be enough for children with "defective genetics" such as MAOA deficiency or XYY. Should operations or medications be allowed as "violence prevention?" This ethical question is similar to that of using "chemical castration" for sex offenses. These approaches go against much of the understanding related to the U.S. Constitution. Lesser standards of protecting individual rights may be invoked when a situation is regarded as "medical." You cannot condemn people, Ms. Andrews said, because they are "potentially dangerous." If violence were medicalized to this extent, a person might be detained or given drugs as a type of "quarantine."

Some genetic considerations already are weighed in the court. For example, a Native American defendant considered to have a genetic propensity to alcoholism received a lighter sentence then he would have without the condition. In another health-related case, pregnant women giving birth at a municipal hospital were tested—without warrants—for cocaine. Those who tested positive were arrested and moved from the court into a treatment program. The requirement for "individualized suspicion" was considered unnecessary because this was a medical intervention. A disturbing trend is emerging in divorce cases in which one spouse seeks an order for genetic testing of the other to determine whether the spouse may have a genetic predisposition toward a condition that may show he or she would be an unfit parent. This information might then be used in custody proceedings. A woman was acquitted of murdering her son after she was tested and diagnosed with Huntington's disease, a hereditary, progressive, degenerative neurological disorder, which was used to demonstrate that she was not "responsible" for the act. Some researchers will testify about such connections. Appropriate decisionmaking, said Ms. Andrews, must address social implications for issues such as custody of children and allow them to be carefully considered.

Question-and-Answer Session
An attendee said that, even for simple diseases, it is hard to attach complex behavior to "a gene." DNA eventually may be used for phenotyping, but Dr. Denno said most geneticists she encoun-

tered "were appalled" at the idea that a "gene for crime" might exist. Dr. H.G. Brunner, who did the research on MAOA deficiency, did not know that the article about his work was being used. She said, however, that some irresponsible scientists would testify—for example, on the probability that a person might kill someone—based on a genetic background. Expectant mothers, if they desired, could be tested for XYY and MAOA deficiency and abort the fetuses if they test positive. A common deterministic view of genetics exists in social institutions (e.g., insurance companies, private businesses, divorce courts).

A judge in the audience asked about studying the prevalence of these genes in the noncriminal population. Dr. Denno said Whitken, in 1976, looked at a large population of Danish men. Only about seven men in Denmark had the genetic combination he sought, and he did not find a link to violence. He did, however, find some link to property crime and some effect on IQ.

Another participant asked about research on existing DNA databanks using informed consent approaches. All offender databases have civil or criminal penalties for any unpermitted use. The presenter panel did not know of any research program of size on these databanks. Ms. Andrews said some States—Indiana, Rhode Island, and Wyoming, for example—will not permit genetic research connected to diseases because of family conflicts over insurance. Another attendee asked about studies of elevated testosterone levels. Dr. Denno said some study had been conducted on elevated testosterone levels as a mitigating factor in relation to rape cases.

Moderator **Margaret Berger**, Suzanne J. and Norman Miles Professor of Law, Brooklyn Law School, New York, brought up the subject of postconviction DNA testing since 1986. These cases have forced some reconceptualization of the law. For considerations of efficiency, economy, and closure, people had been used to thinking that a convicted person had received constitutional guarantees and a just result through the trial process. Protocols for keeping and using evidence in State laboratories and prosecutors' offices are changing, too. This area requires careful thought about the use of resources. DNA evidence has undercut the finality of decisions and the idea that convictions are "accurate"; as a result, a demand on judicial resources for retrying old cases with newly discovered DNA evidence puts a strain on already overburdened court dockets. The use of DNA evidence also is responsible for more rigorous scientific standards in such areas as fingerprinting and eyewitness testimony. It has stimulated interest in finding the "real perpetrators" through DNA databanks.

The constitutional framework is shifting, Ms. Berger continued, and people must consider the rights of indigents. More legislation is being considered in many States to give convicted persons the right to DNA testing; this is not "new evidence" but rather an access to evidence not previously available. Few cases turn out to be "true exonerations." Mostly, some evidence is shown to be weak or unfair, but the impact at trial could have been significant.

Panel VIII. New Procedures for Identification

George Clarke, deputy district attorney, San Diego, California, referred to new "interfaces" of scientific evidence with courtroom procedures. The *Frye* rule, he said, was concerned about the misleading aura of certainty in scientific evidence that might lead too easily to conviction. In California, in adhering to the *Kelly* [*People* v. *Kelly*, 549 P.2d 1240 (Cal. 1976)]/*Frye* standard, the appellate court decided not to hold admissibility hearings on PCR-based DNA evidence; in essence the "customers" were satisfied that the typing methodology worked. In other States, such as in Georgia, trial judges have been told "not to make determination" of scientific reliability.

Cassandra Calloway, senior research associate in human genetics, Roche Molecular Systems/ Children's Hospital Oakland Research Institute, Alameda, California, spoke about how mitochondrial DNA (mtDNA) technology is rapidly finding its way into laboratories around the Nation. Newer analytical methods using mtDNA allow screening of up to 40 samples in 3 hours, easy interpretation either visually or with simple software, conservation of sample material using duplex amplification, and an established technology available to any laboratory. Nuclear DNA— needed for the old method of testing—is a much larger molecule and unique to each individual. Analysis requires a relatively large sample in good condition. Why, then, should mtDNA be used? It is a much smaller molecule, said Ms. Calloway, and thousands of copies are present in any cell from an individual. Unlike nuclear DNA, which is passed on from both mother and father, mtDNA is maternally inherited, and samples that are degraded or unusually small can still be used effectively by comparing them with any maternal relative of the person authorities suspect may have left the sample.

The D-loop of mtDNA—the noncoding portion of the molecule—is highly variable among individuals. These hypervariable regions are used by the forensic community. Samples with insufficient nuclear DNA, such as hairs, can still be successfully used for identification. The time for analysis of mtDNA is also much quicker. Laboratories can simultaneously amplify two regions of the sample, with one chemical reaction, reducing the number of necessary sequencing efforts. The probe will bind only to the correct sequence in the sample. Matching with the complimentary, hybridized probe can easily be interpreted.

In contrast to analyzing the nuclear DNA sequence, which can take 3 days, sequence-specific oligonucleotide (SSO) typing with mtDNA can be completed in 3 hours. This technique was introduced in court in 1990 and has been broadly accepted. Papers have been published on the methods, which use the same equipment as original immobilized SSO assays in the past. Using the technique, it is easy to exclude a person's DNA sample when it does not match key evidence. The method also has been successfully used to identify human remains found after the battles in Croatia.

Colin Smithpeter, technical staff, Sandia National Laboratories, Albuquerque, New Mexico, presented information on a new camera technology aimed at improving crime scene investigations. The unit has a base, tripod, active light source, and LCD (liquid crystal display) screen. In the past, investigators have relied on 35mm cameras and secondary light sources. The new camera can find translucent biological stains in a number of difficult field conditions. The developers continue to work to improve the equipment's sensitivity and ability to reject ambient light. In all cases in which the camera has been tested, it was able to find stains invisible to current techniques. It finds stains on skin as well, and the camera can document splatter patterns for later analysis or presentation in court.

The camera uses scattered light imaging to find untreated fingerprints on a variety of surfaces, such as glass windows, plastic garbage bags, sides of a pistol, plastic security cards, or computer floppy disks. The technology is more limited when the surface is rough and porous and when ambient light is too great. The technology has also been useful in examining gunshot residues, which can be extremely specific. A crime scene videotaped by the camera can yield evidence that may not at first be considered important. Cases in which the technology has been used include an armed robbery and a rape/murder investigation. The outlook for the equipment depends on establishing commercial partnerships to miniaturize and manufacture the equipment. It also needs further developmental work to improve fingerprint imaging and more validation for admissibility of data into court.

Question-and-Answer Session

An audience member asked about DNA analysis for individuals who are heteroplasmic, or have more than one mtDNA type. Ms. Calloway responded that difficult cases, such as those in which a person has heteroplasmy, need to be confirmed by other sequencing techniques. Regardless of typing methods, some problems with heteroplasmy can occur. At George Mason University, researchers are working with the Federal Bureau of Investigation (FBI) to sequence 5,000 individuals using SSO technology to establish a database. Mr. Clarke added that, similar to the area of serology, type analysis has to be considered in the interpretation process. Training scientists in interpretation is an important part of the process. Heteroplasmy can be compared with contamination in a sample. It might even help a case when a match is found because it is rare.

A participant asked about British analytical work using shed cells from fingerprints. Dr. Smithpeter said the new technology would have a less destructive effect on traces of fingerprints than the currently used powders. Another attendee asked about variable wavelengths of light in connection with the new camera equipment: Had tests been conducted using multiple wavelengths? Dr. Smithpeter said a number of filters for different wavelengths are available for the equipment to maximize the information captured by the technician.

Luncheon Presentation: Stalking—The Science, the Law, and Courtroom Dynamics

J. Reid Meloy, forensic psychologist, San Diego, California, said the first stalking laws were passed in California in 1990. Stalking is a relatively new area of criminology, and several constitutional challenges have been made. Delineation of a stalking crime requires a "pattern," a "threat," and demonstration of fear in the victim.

About 8 percent of American females report being stalked at some time in their lives, most frequently when they are in their thirties. Immigration has been found to be a risk factor. Stalkers tend to have a higher intelligence level that exhibits itself in creative/manipulative behavior, prior criminal or psychiatric experiences, and drug abuse histories. They also are often unemployed or underemployed; and treatment of a stalking offender has indicated that employment favors psychological improvement.

Dr. Meloy described a typology of stalkers as the following:

- *Erotomanic:* those who are convinced they are "loved by the other" (approximately 10 percent).

- *Love obsessional:* those who are convinced of the existence of a relationship although they are a stranger to the object person (about 28 percent).
- *Simple obsessional:* those who have had some type of relationship with the object person (approximately 60 percent).
- *"False victims":* those who claim they are themselves the object of retaliation or psychotic behavior from the object person (around 2 percent).

In Australia, another typology—the Mullen—has been developed, which distinguishes the following types of stalkers:

- Persons rejected by an existing relationship.
- Intimacy seekers.
- Persons who are socially incompetent.
- Resentful persons.
- Predators, more than half of whom are violent.

Violence associated with stalking, said Dr. Meloy, most often does not involve a weapon, nor does it often involve injury that requires medical attention. The most common mental disorders among stalkers are Axis II, or narcissistic, antisocial personality disorders. Fifty to seventy percent of inmates in any jail or prison exhibit this type of disorder.

Stalkers who pursue public figures are more likely to be psychotic than those who pursue private citizens, but less than 2 percent use guns or violence or commit homicide. Stalkers who pursue private individuals, however, are less likely to be psychotic, but they are more likely to use threats or violence and to commit homicide. These acts are considered "affective," not mentally disordered.

Dr. Meloy described stalking as "surprisingly nonsexual." Rather than being triggered by envy, more often it is the result of easily punctured pride and wrath that masks the shame of rejection. American popular culture and the media tacitly sanction forms of stalking behavior through the promotion of such products as the fragrance "Obsession" or popular activities labeled "mania" (e.g., Elvis mania).

Panel IX. Call-for-Papers Presentations

Renegotiating Science: Fingerprinting and Daubert

Simon Cole, visualization architect, Visual Networks, Brooklyn, New York, spoke about the courts' dilemma regarding fingerprint evidence, which is increasingly regarded as "not scientific" and unreliable. The paradox arises out of conflicting notions of scientific knowledge. One belief is that "truly scientific" knowledge should provide greater certainty than "ordinary evidence." The early practice of fingerprinting in connection with investigations fit with this idea, and matches were framed to the courts as "facts." It was generally accepted that no two people have the same fingerprints; therefore, unique identification could be confirmed.

After *Daubert*, Dr. Cole commented, this orthodoxy was questioned. Fingerprint examiners, it was argued, do not have methods for exposing errors or falsification. The *Daubert* court said there were no certainties in science, only probabilistic results. Forensic fingerprint identification came under fire; even the same finger will not produce exactly the same print twice in a row. The impression of a small area of a fingerprint may match any number of different fingers. Since then, fingerprinting methodology has added proficiency testing and new qualitative and quantitative analysis. The science has had to "reconstruct itself," an example of how law and the scientific world play active roles in mutual development.

Paul Sarmousakis, an assistant U.S. attorney in Philadelphia, who was in the audience, recalled the first *Daubert* hearing on fingerprint evidence, which took place in Philadelphia in July 1999. Only a handful of people have raised this issue to date; most feel it is ludicrous that "fingerprints are not valid." *Daubert* only tells judges they are bound by Federal Rules of Evidence, specifically Rule 702, and suggests criteria to determine if evidence should be admissible. *Daubert* emphasizes rigorous testing and organized skepticism.

Mr. Steven Meagher, an audience member who is with the latent print unit of the FBI, said Dr. Cole's paper represents an ongoing debate. In all hearings, judges will rule on what evidence is admissible. In Indiana, one judicial opinion stated, "[I]n sum, despite absence of a quantifiable standard, the court is satisfied that latent print identification is reliable expert evidence." Another participant added that opinions support both sides of the argument, which is an example of how *Daubert* has confused the judiciary.

Trace Evidence: Evaluating Significance and Validity When There Are No Hard Numbers
Chesterene Cwiklik, faculty, Pacific Coast Forensic Science Institute, Seattle, Washington, asked the group to think about what should be done in situations in which no database is available for statistical analysis. Trace evidence reflects the processes, creatures, activities, geography, and season that produced it. Because trace evidence often is not stable over time, courts have a hard time evaluating it.

Good science, stated Ms. Cwiklik, involves an articulated hypothesis, test and analysis, and interpretation of the results. For accurate association and identification, three processes have to be systematic:

- Establishing criteria for correspondence.
- Collecting information about occurrence and transfer.
- Formulating and testing alternate (sorted) hypotheses.

There are always real-life limitations to the quality and size of samples, but it is possible to address the reliability of testing methods in terms of error rates. The "refutationist approach" is also valuable: Can the explanation stand up to a rigorous critique? What other explanations fit the data? All this is testable. Science uses inductive process (fact gathering) and deductive process (testing of theories) to arrive at the most probable conclusions.

The Effects of **Daubert v. Merrell Dow Pharmaceuticals** *on the Admissibility of Expert Testimony in State and Federal Criminal Cases*
Jennifer Groscup, research assistant, Law/Psychology Program, University of Nebraska-Lincoln, presented information on a study containing more than 100 variables to clarify which

factors have affected criminal appellate decisions and content analysis since *Daubert*. The case experts were in the medical, mental health, technical (e.g., police procedure), engineering, and scientific (e.g., chemist, geneticist) fields. Since the *Daubert* decision, according to the study, the discussion devoted to *Frye* has decreased. The mean number of words shows more exchange about scientific topics than about technical, medical, or business ones. The project selected an equal number of Federal and State appeals cases, 66 percent before *Daubert* and 34 percent after the decision. Generally, defendants were appealing the admission of a prosecution expert, but sometimes the defense was appealing the exclusion of its own expert.

What factors, asked Ms. Groscup, most affected admissibility of evidence? The study used a multivariate model in which admissibility was a dependent variable. This allows people to see how judgment criteria are used over time. In general, technical testimony has been viewed as "more likely to assist"; scientific testimony has been considered "less likely to assist." Courts have thought that technical testimony, such as police experience and investigative technique, was relevant and helpful to decisionmakers but that scientific testimony was more likely to be "prejudicial and not helpful to the trier of fact." Judges have been more likely to use the reliability criteria in connection with scientific testimony.

No great revolution has followed the *Daubert* decision, Ms. Groscup concluded. Federal Rules of Evidence Rule 702 is more likely than any other rule to be discussed, but not in terms of specific criteria under *Daubert*. The Federal Rules of Evidence still drive most admissibility decisions.

"Matches" an Overinference of Data? A Giglio Obligation?
Frederic Whitehurst, executive director, Forensic Justice Project, Washington, D.C., said that DNA analysis has shown that the jury system is not free from error. No one would willingly put an innocent person in jail; the responsibility we have, he added, is to find the errors. In particular, it is important not to "overinfer" the data. An expert should at least alert the trier of fact or a litigating lawyer that there are numerous factors to consider and that conclusions that are not supported by the data should not be stated.

Dr. Whitehurst posed the example of forensic paint analysis in which the human eye is subject to errors concerning subtle differences. Analysts have to proceed further and look at the samples of crystalline components, considering specific elements with infrared analysis and chromatography. They may need to decompose some of the material under high heat, check resulting gases, and use a spectrometer to see which compounds are indicated. Even then, errors may occur when determining if the samples are from the same paint. When a technician says a sample "is the same" even though there is still considerable uncertainty, it introduces error into the system.

Panel X. Breakout Sessions
Ensuring Quality Standards in Forensic Science Laboratories
Michael Sheppo, bureau chief, Illinois State Police, Springfield, spoke about the impact that quality standards have in forensic science laboratories. He concentrated most of his presentation on standards of the American Society of Crime Laboratory Directors (ASCLD) and the Illinois State Police. He spoke about the different ways in which ASCLD takes action to influence and produce change, ensuring that quality forensic science services are provided nationwide. Some

key issues are funding for the improvement of crime laboratory facilities, replacing outmoded equipment, and expanding training programs for scientists. Other issues include pursuing changes in legislation and policy, such as enhancing areas and standards of accreditation and increasing timeliness of services, to improve the laboratory work product and maximize case solvability and prosecution. Mr. Sheppo discussed in detail the Illinois State Police's Division of Forensic Services, Forensic Sciences Command, and how it uses proficiency testing as a quality assurance measure. He said that proficiency tests should examine a laboratory's total quality system, including evidence receipts, analysis, administrative review, and results reports.

According to Mr. Sheppo, two types of analytical skills should be tested: basic and complex. Basic skills include tests for common analytes and routine casework. Complex skills include infrequently encountered analytes and difficult casework that may need specialized techniques. He pointed out that proficiency tests can be handled the same as casework but should not be subject to policies adopted for purposes of efficiency or expediency. When an analyst knows a sample is a proficiency test, the analyst may take more care than is typical for normal casework.

William Tilstone, executive director, National Forensic Science Technology Center (NFSTC), Largo, Florida, discussed other aspects of quality assurance, such as training, systems, method validations, controls and standards used in testing, and equipment calibration and maintenance. He spent the majority of his presentation discussing the use of standards, which he defined as "a material of assured analyte content." Standards are used to calibrate instrument response, validate new methods or changes in methods, and measure analyst competency once training is completed. NFSTC's Quality Sample Program provides a range of secondary standards.

Dr. Tilstone discussed how samples are manufactured and quality control is checked using NFSTC's method. The samples are distributed in sealed containers, labeled with a code, and placed in a sealed envelope addressed to the quality manager. Proficiency tests and reference standards are performed to measure and improve quality. The two key questions, said Dr. Tilstone, are:

- Is there effective evaluation of the root cause for an error?
- If so, has effective corrective action been implemented?

The Law's Treatment of Medical Expertise: The Roles of Clinical Judgment and Epidemiological Research

Barbara Hulka, Kenan Professor of Epidemiology, University of North Carolina at Chapel Hill, spoke about the variations in method between scientific and legal disciplines. In science, typically:

- A scientist posits a theory or hypothesis.
- The scientist tests the hypothesis.
- Data refutes or supports the scientist's hypothesis.
- The scientist consults, communicates, or collaborates with others about his or her testing process.

In the legal world, however:

- Truth about disputed circumstances is determined by the jury.
- The system is adversarial in nature.
- Paid experts work with each side.
- Scientists often are hesitant to testify.

Dr. Hulka was asked to collaborate on a National Academy of Sciences panel on silicone breast implants. The panel was assembled to provide neutral, unbiased information on technical subjects to the judiciary for a huge class action case. The panel analyzed scientific literature on the causal relation between silicone breast implants and connective tissue diseases. Panel members looked at more than 2,000 documents from both sides. Each side of the litigation had a special liaison counsel to the panel. Many experts were disposed about methods in their respective fields and described those methods in terms selected to ensure the jury's understanding. Analysis strategies and risk exposure were considered using epidemiological and meta-analytical studies.

The panel, explained Dr. Hulka, used meta-analysis to group, compare, and summarize available data on selected diseases. It made best estimates both using and leaving out Hennekens' study of 400,000 women—far larger than the other compared studies—in the calculations, so that overemphasis of its results could be judged. No meaningful or consistent association of the diseases with breast implants was found with a broad confidence interval. Other large, highly visible cases considering complex technical or scientific questions, Dr. Hulka concluded, may be interested in establishing court-appointed science panels of this type.

Gregg Bloche, professor, Georgetown University Law Center, and adjunct professor, Department of Health Policy and Management, Johns Hopkins University, Washington, D.C., spoke about the idea of neutral experts and "truth determination." Judges worry that normative biases will be reflected in the work of scientific experts. The process of cross-examination is intended to shed light on this, but it may not help the court reach a decision.

Dr. Bloche gave as an example the case of C. Kennedy, who developed symptoms of lupus after injections of Xyderm for cosmetic purposes. Elevated antibodies connected to injections of bovine collagen were found to be "associated" with symptoms but not "causal." In other words, science alone was not enough to show causation in the case. Relationships may be only temporal or circumstantial, be caused by more or less likely alternative causes, and have clearer causality, using reasoning by analogy. Disputes among experts reflect a pervasive argument concerning uncertainties that face physicians and other professionals.

The question of whether doctors' work is efficacious, said Dr. Bloche, is a bigger problem than causation. What should reasonable health care cover to be "efficacious?" A parallel can be seen between the judicial skeptic and the health care provider that is reluctant to pay. The consideration of what "necessary treatment," including a cost-benefit aspect, means involves conflicts similar to those faced in judging a person's competence to stand trial in cases of the "insanity defense." When child custody is involved, practicing mental health professionals often recommend one parent as being "better" than the other. About 90 percent of the time, courts will follow this advice, although profound philosophical or responsibility questions may persist. The difficulty of such judgments explains the wide "de facto" differences in legal standards.

A participant asked the presenters to comment on doubts surrounding experts because of financial incentives. From the audience, a forensic scientist responded that, in about 40 percent of the cases referred to him, his expertise was not welcome because it did not contribute to the client's case. A staff member from Duke University described the registry, or database, of independent expert advisers that the school is creating. This resource is intended to be used for complex legal disputes and to reduce concerns about bias in retaining experts.

Saturday, October 14, 2000

Introduction to the Clutter Murder Case

Donald Bersoff, director, Law and Psychology Program, Villanova University School of Law and Medical College of Pennsylvania/Hahnemann University, explained that the third day of the conference would focus on evidence from the Clutter murder case from the 1950s and 1960s and how treatment of evidence had changed in the intervening years and what would be admitted to the court today.

In November 1959, Perry Smith and Dick Hickock attempted to rob the home of Herb and Bonnie Clutter in Holcomb, Kansas. In particular, Smith and Hickock were looking for a safe that Mr. Clutter supposedly kept in his office. Unable to locate the safe, Smith and Hickock killed the Clutters (including their two children), all of whom were awakened during the attempted robbery. The two men were convicted of first-degree murder in 1960 and, after several appeals in the State of Kansas and to the U.S. Supreme Court, were hung to death in April 1965.

Truman Capote, who was employed at the time by the *New York Times*, was interested in the story. He went to Kansas and stayed for 5 years. His book *In Cold Blood* was published the same year the two men were executed. Since then, a movie, a miniseries, a documentary, and several research papers related to the murder case have been produced.

Jennifer Evans Marsh, attorney and psychologist, Federal Judicial Center, Washington, D.C., set the scene of the murder case for the audience, reminding them that it was the period of President Eisenhower and the Warren Court. The two defendants had implicated themselves in their confessions and in the disclosure of the location of further evidence. Major pieces of evidence at the crime scene included a purse, footprints, cut telephone cords, and Herbert Clutter's wallet. Evidence located elsewhere were a box containing boots with blood on them, a shotgun and knife from one of the defendant's houses, and a radio. Testimony from a gas station attendant and a former cellmate of one of the defendants also pointed to their guilt.

Presentations during the morning conference sessions focused on physical evidence; afternoon sessions centered on psychology and admissibility. During each session, a representative from the scientific community discussed the evidence; prosecutors and public defenders followed the scientific discussion with legal comments.

Larry Thomas, special agent in charge, Kansas Bureau of Investigation, Topeka, told the attendees that defendant Perry Smith wanted the story of the Clutter family murder written "so other people would not make the same mistakes."

The Clutters, explained Mr. Thomas, were "low-risk victims," what might be termed pillars of the community. Their murders made the national press, with extensive coverage by the *New York Times* and the *Washington Post*. Herbert Clutter was an active leader in the farming community. His wife, Bonnie, had recently been diagnosed with depression and was about to receive medical treatment. The daughter, Nancy, a high school student, was extremely well liked and, on the day of the murder, had helped a neighbor make cherry pie. The son, Kenyon, had spent that day making an oak chest for his sister's wedding. Two older sisters were married and lived away from home.

Panel XI. Blood and DNA Evidence

Lisa Forman, Acting Director, Investigative and Forensic Sciences Division, Office of Science and Technology, NIJ, said she and Anjali Swienton, also at NIJ, had earlier worked for Cellmark Diagnostics, a DNA testing company, at which they gained considerable experience working with and presenting DNA evidence.

DNA's organic molecular structure, Dr. Forman said, is arranged in a ladder (a double helix) and contains individuals' genetic information. In the same sense that a word, synonym, sentence, chapter, and book hold information, so do the codon, allele, gene, chromosome, and genome of DNA. No two people share exactly the same arrangement of the 3 billion base pairs, not even identical twins. However, 99.9 percent of all people's DNA is indistinguishable; the 0.1 percent that differs is referred to as "DNA markers."

For forensic purposes, RFLP analysis of nuclear DNA has been done since 1989. It requires a relatively large sample, about 1,000 cells of good quality. This testing has been done by FBI standards and has good courtroom reliability, but it is labor intensive and slow. Dr. Forman explained that the newer technology uses STR markers and PCR, which is like a genetic "Xeroxing process" that makes multiple copies of the DNA present in a sample. The reaction can be performed with only 30 cells and can be semiautomated. Routinely, the analysis uses 13 STR markers, each with about 7 alleles, or "synonyms." These give a high power of discrimination when used in combination to create a DNA "profile."

In the Clutter case, the rope, tape, and hair could have been screened for DNA had the technology been available. Because the two defendants had served time, in a modern investigation their DNA might have been found in the FBI's CODIS database. Evidence from the gun and knife could have been used, and sufficient blood could have been lifted from the recovered boots of Smith and Hickock for DNA analysis.

David Meier, chief, Homicide Unit, Suffolk County DA's Office, Boston, Massachusetts, gave the group an overview of a prosecutor's approach to the Clutter case in a modern timeframe. In Capote's description of the case, an overwhelming impression of guilt is presupposed, but what, asked Mr. Meier, if the defendants had not given incriminating evidence against themselves? It can be hard to convince 12 lay people of guilt "beyond a reasonable doubt." Before the testimony of former cellmate Floyd Wells, the only solid evidence available to the prosecution was the bootprints.

Today, more than 40 years later, the processing of the crime scene at the farm might have taken 6 or 7 days, which is longer than the original trial. In Meier's jurisdiction (Boston), he is paged whenever a homicide occurs, 24 hours a day. His crime scene role in a case such as the Clutters would be minimal, but it would be important in terms of coordination and communication. He would assemble the best investigators and laboratory technicians for the crime scene evidence and would ensure that different law enforcement offices work together.

When the prosecutor offers evidence to the jury, he or she is not only identifying the defendant but trying to determine what has happened. Defendants Smith and Hickock engaged in finger-pointing, each claiming he was less responsible than the other. These considerations are important at sentencing. Had DNA typing been available, Mr. Meier said, the prosecution could have determined which person was at a particular site. The case might have justified an application for a warrant to keep nonessential people out of the area to keep them from contaminating the scene and to allow investigators and technicians to process the evidence.

Without confessions, the prosecutor may have tried to collect DNA from the suspects. This type of evidence—getting DNA samples from evidence such as soda cans or cigarette butts—has been upheld in the courts when they find "probable cause." In general, the prosecution requests as much scientific testing as possible before evidence degrades and becomes less useful. Typically, the defense questions many of the tests, challenges sufficiency of the samples, or claims that other tests should be done. An important question is whether the expert's laboratory is open to counsel to review visual aids for presenting the case. Mr. Meier recommended traveling to the expert's laboratory to review testimony and discuss themes of the case with the expert prior to presenting testimony.

Rita Fry, public defender, Cook County Public Defender's Office, Chicago, Illinois, discussed how trial standards for defense have changed since the Clutter trial. New standards for effective assistance of counsel require that the defending attorney be as well prepared as the prosecution in dealing with such scientific issues as DNA analysis.

For example, some inconsistencies in treatment of blood samples are found in a police report. A blood sample was collected from the garage but not kept. The defense should question whether the evidence has been contaminated and whether additional evidence should have been reviewed but was missed. DNA analysis methods have varying requirements for the samples, and time delays in analyzing the samples are significant. If defense counsel discovers that DNA analysis standards were not followed properly or that time delays were significant, it should consider effects of the failure to follow standards or of the time delays on the DNA results.

Under discovery rules, the defense must be able to talk to the scientists who are testing the samples; the scientists should be neutral and not focused on making a certain determination relative to the case. Because prosecutors bear the burden of proving guilt, scientists should be able to answer questions about the credentials of the laboratory or about comparisons to national requirements. Crime laboratories sometimes are operated by law enforcement and might be viewed as favoring the prosecution.

A strong case often can be made that an expert is a "hired gun" who testifies to anything for the right price. Defense counsel should, for example, properly check whether an expert has financial contracts to the laboratory where testing is conducted. Because of an Illinois decision concerning persons on death row, most defender offices now have budgets for expert witnesses. Both sides also should consider review by independent laboratories. Scientists should appreciate that cross-examination is not personal; it is necessary to attempt to obtain a fair and just result. In the Clutter case, without the confessions, almost no clear evidence was found, not even the shotgun shells. Today, Ms. Fry said, the defendants Hickock and Smith would be considered to have received improper defense at trial.

In open discussion, a laboratory scientist in the audience noted that analysts need prosecutors to tell them what is considered probative so they can target useful evidence. Another participant said that, as the case progresses, emerging evidence may be important for either side. For example, cleaning a shotgun could prove "presence of mind."

Panel XII. Firearms and Toolmarks

Lucien Haag, president, Forensic Sciences Services, Inc., Carefree, Arizona, described the use of shot shells, wadding, and projectiles as means of identifying guns used in shootings. In the Clutter case, little shot shell wadding was recovered from the victims, and no propellant residue was collected during the autopsies. Identification aids would have been limited to head stamps on the cartridges and brand identification on the wadding. Traces of blood in the shotgun bore and examples of shot and wadding found could have been used in reconstructing the crime; for example, using characteristics of the wounds produced to determine the range at which the victims were shot. In addition, the wadding may be marked by peculiarities on the gun, such as the site piece drilled through the bore on some weapons.

Amie Clifford, assistant director, National College of District Attorneys, Columbia, South Carolina, spoke about the prosecution's tasks. Lawyers usually do not learn about forensics in law school. The prosecutor has to educate himself or herself about the science or technique involved and, most important, about communicating key aspects of the evidence to the jury. The prosecutor needs to review the evidence and case theory with the expert and use the expert's exact terminology when speaking about that testimony. The FBI offers a handbook on forensic services and other references on its Web site (*www.fbi.gov/hq/lab/fsc/current/search.htm*).

Henry Hall, head deputy, Special Trials Unit, Alternate Public Defender's Office, Los Angeles, California, said it is important to look at the evidence from both a scientific and a lay person's point of view. Such details as blood type make a hard, clear impression on a jury, while other points may be "soft" and more interpretive. In an area of expertise that involves such interpretation, the expert cannot have "been given an opinion" in advance. For example, the prosecution may not give an expert a letter favoring a certain interpretation before the analysis is complete. In discovery, the defense can get the laboratory or bench notes to learn how the evidence was put together. Firearms evidence, for example, can be microscopic; the defense can question whether it was handled carefully enough.

In the Clutter case, confessions and corroboration were obtained, so the defense might focus on the penalty phase and sentencing. Descriptions of the shooting ("the room went blue") give rise to many psychological issues that might lead a jury to think this was not a cold-blooded killing. The defense might look at the shotgun trigger to see if it had a "light trigger pull" and to consider the effect of the noise on a defendant who could be having a psychological episode.

Question-and-Answer Session
A participant asked if a variety of experts would be needed to give a wound pattern analysis. Mr. Hall said that presenter Haag was a particularly trustworthy example, but sometimes the attorney will look for a coroner or retired homicide detective to discuss his or her experience.

Another participant asked if there were advantages to having a bench trial and forgoing the jury. Ms. Clifford responded that both sides would have to agree on this, and it seldom occurs. A bench trial, however, may be held to "avoid compassion in the jury."

An attendee asked about the efficiency of computerized programs that match weapons and firearms evidence. Mr. Haag said the larger government laboratories have wonderful systems, similar to IAFIS (Integrated Automated Fingerprint Identification System), but a human examiner will still need to look at the components and make a conclusion. Mr. Hall, speaking about Los Angeles in the aftermath of the "Ramparts" police scandal, said that the entire DRUGFIRE database on firearms evidence had been called into question.

Another participant asked if inappropriate rounds might sometimes be used in a gun, making matching hard or impossible. Mr. Haag said this would be unusual, and the weapon would be unlikely to work properly. In the Clutter case, a mechanically operated gun was used; it was "a little crazy" for someone to pick up shells and clean this type of gun.

Panel XIII. Trace Evidence: Footprints

William Bodziak, Forensic Consultant Services, and retired special agent, Federal Bureau of Investigation, Jacksonville, Florida, said footprints at the Clutter home were destroyed in the process of crime scene personnel's investigation of the scene. Other parts of the house were not examined for prints; today, many more prints would have been recovered.

When eight consecutive bloody footprints are left, Mr. Bodziak explained, the fourth to the eighth prints usually contain more detailed information than the first and second prints. The FBI did not mention that Smith had resoled his boot prior to being found, which would have created unique nail markings in the print. The diamond print left by Hickock also was not listed in the reports, although Smith and Hickock were arrested within 5 minutes of repossessing the footwear (both pairs of boots were in a package Smith sent to himself from Mexico). Using the footwear, much more could have been done to corroborate the defendants' stories.

Mitchell Benson, executive assistant district attorney, chief of trials, Homicide Bureau, Kings County DA's Office, Brooklyn, New York, contrasted the Brooklyn courtrooms to the usually orderly processes of science. He agreed with the other prosecutors that he would focus on the defendants' statements as he pursued the case. The physical exhibits would be important corroborative tools, and investigators would testify on the preservation and chain of custody of DNA, ballistics, and footwear evidence.

Although DNA may establish that the defendants committed the crime, Mr. Benson said, the jury's understanding is critical. If expert testimony is too scientific or complicated, the jury may not be able to follow it. If the expert is challenged, the jurors may lose sight of the evidence's importance and question the expert's trustworthiness.

Jeffrey Thoma, public defender, Mendocino County, California (Ukiah), told the participants that the defense would remind jurors of what had *not* been done. The defense would probably try to keep the footwear evidence out of the court, challenge the connections of time and place, and remind the jury of all the people who had access to the home: friends, relatives, and officials.

Footwear examiners, said Mr. Thoma, come from diverse backgrounds. It might be possible to question whether the impression was good enough to conclude a match. Many pairs of the same model of shoe would have been sold in the region. A bare footprint might leave ridge information. In today's litigation, looking at how the impression was lifted also is crucial. A microscopic examination could be ordered.

Luncheon Presentation: The Truth May Be Out There—Forensic Science Meets the Television Industry

Paul Rabwin, producer, "The X-Files," 20th Century Fox Television, Los Angeles, California, said he had first signed to produce the program in 1993. The show added an FBI adviser (among others) to check ideas for episodes. Mr. Rabwin complemented the work of Mr. Capote, saying it was "as good as any courtroom script," then showed the group some selections of "TV science."

Surprising and small cultural and language issues, said Mr. Rabwin, have to be worked out for good TV representation. For example, when filming at a Canadian site, a local actress had never heard of S'mores, the popular U.S. campfire snack. In another example, a father and daughter were supposed to be speaking Cantonese, but the actors spoke another Chinese dialect. For this program, Mr. Rabwin said, they rerecorded every line with a Cantonese language adviser so as not to offend the Cantonese-speaking community.

Forensic academies sometimes want to "scold me," he related. "We field plenty of calls, but we do try to keep the program in tune with what law enforcement and forensics are doing. We contact experts for every show." The show has many medical advisers, such as operating room nurses and college professors, to check the medical facts.

During the open-question session, a person asked him why the episodes have been "so dark." This was a stylistic decision, Mr. Rabwin responded. It is scarier and more dramatic if viewers do not see things clearly and are allowed to let their imaginations work.

Panel XIV. Trace Evidence: Rope and Tape

John Thornton, senior forensic scientist, Forensic Science Division, Forensic Analytical, Hayward, California, spoke about developing data before submission of evidence. In the Clutter case, the victims had been bound with two-inch fabric-type surgical tape with nylon cord such as that used for parachutes. The latter is widely available and extremely strong: it must be cut, not broken. It also was a type of cord not often used on farms. Had investigators known this type of cord would have to be cut with a knife, it might have helped to sequence events.

Other tape and cordage was later found in a ditch. The items were buried rather deep—earth-moving equipment was needed to remove them. In observable features, the materials matched that found with the victims. The morphology—color, diameter, braid—could have been compared. If this evidence was found within the past year, infrared analysis might have been conducted for more rigorous identification, or pyrolysis and gas chromatography might have been used to distinguish the make of the nylon. There currently are also many more manufacturers of adhesive tape—approximately 4,000 manufacturers have Web sites—than at the time of these murders. Most convincing for the conviction was the "devastating" match of the tear ends of the tape found at the scene with the tape found in the ditch. The thread count matched, and such a tear could never be duplicated.

Mr. Benson spoke again about the prosecution's actions in connection with the evidence. He would ensure that his expert had the right credentials and specialization to give an opinion to the jury. In this case, where the evidence is so strong, the length of presentation of the case may be important. Avoiding some scientific discussion may be valuable, rather than subjecting the jury members to too much elaboration.

Mr. Thoma acknowledged that this evidence would be difficult for the defense case. The exact fits of the torn tape and rope ends would "perfect" the picture in a lay person's eyes. In general, defense counsel might seek the expert's bench notes to determine if the expert testimony could be excluded. It can be an onerous expense for the defense to strongly pursue discovery on the forensics, but it is crucial. The defense needs to know as much as possible about the science behind the evidence, possibly even more than the prosecutor. Networking among defense attorneys concerning expert testimony and neutral analysis is increasing.

During open discussion, Dr. Thornton pointed out that while blood evidence has undergone a paradigm shift, analysis of the cords and tape evidence has not changed much. An audience member asked about the availability of expert advice to small jurisdictions. Mr. Thoma, whose jurisdiction is small and nonurban, said he juggles resources so he can consult experts on important cases.

Panel XV. Psychiatric and Psychological Evidence

Norman Poythress, professor, Department of Mental Health Law & Policy, University of South Florida, Tampa, said that the psychological evidence in the Clutter case probably would be most relevant to mitigating circumstances. In the intervening time period, the concept of "competent to stand trial" has undergone great change. In 1959, there were no tools to evaluate the defendants' competence, and there is no record of what the commission doctors actually did with Smith and Hickock. There were no ties to the defendants' "legal abilities" or capacity for legal performance. Psychological tools became more precise when posing the following question: Can this person do what is required for trial?

Still, Dr. Poythress said, many tests are not standardized in important ways, and potential clinician subjectivity in the measures exists. Defendants often are not tested for reasoning tasks that may be important in the decision to plea bargain. In today's setting, the Clutter appeal, which said the trial did not explicitly address sanity, would probably have succeeded. Kansas uses a balancing structure of mitigating and aggravating factors. Five or six of these relate to mental ability.

Michael McCann, district attorney, Milwaukee County, Milwaukee, Wisconsin, said that in the 13th century, the "idiocy" defense was used to mitigate punishment, and the defendant was considered "no more than an infant or wild beast." The state of the law remained much the same for a long time. The state has been allowed to place the burden of proof of insanity on the defendant; jurors were told to presume sanity until the contrary could be proved. Neither "insanity at the time of the act" nor "disease of the mind" were available claims in the 1960s in Kansas.

In the Clutter case, three psychiatrists were appointed to give a competency test, but the insanity test was refused. The judge instead appointed "three physicians and surgeons" who spent a few hours with the defendants and told the judge they were competent. The defense tried to have Dr. W. Mitchell Jones admitted to speak about Hickock's neurological damage, which might have substantially affected his behavior. The lengthy interview with Smith, which revealed serious organic damage and a "horrible social background"—parents parted in violence, two family suicides, orphanages, trouble with the law—seemed to indicate Smith might be schizophrenic. Although the intent was clear in the Clutter case—Hickock repeated often to "leave no witnesses," and the defendants concealed their faces and burned gloves, among other actions—a defense case today would want to ensure that psychiatric evaluation and any possible genetic testing were entered into the record.

Charles Sevilla, former president, California Attorneys for Criminal Justice, San Diego, noted that *Miranda* was not around when these men were interrogated, although they were informed of their rights and waived them. Mental health professionals have testified that "profile evidence" (i.e., an offender fits a specific profile, such as a pedophile, stalker, or serial killer) sometimes can be an aggravating factor for penalties as well as for mitigation. In the 1970s and 1980s, policy showed a swing against "mental defenses" and legislatures acted to make them more difficult to present.

In reality, said Mr. Sevilla, the crazier the person, the *less* likely it is that the mental illness defense will succeed. For example:

- Richard Chase, who became known as the Vampire Killer because he drained and drank the blood of his six victims, was sentenced to death in 1978.
- Dan White, who "executed" the mayor of San Francisco, George Moscone, and city supervisor Harvey Milk in 1978, was convicted of manslaughter because of diminished capacity.
- O.J. Simpson, whose mental state was never raised, was found not guilty.

At the time of the Clutter case, mental health defenses were "in infancy" and defense attorneys were not using psychiatrists. Fears existed that offenders would be released improperly, the criminal justice system would be showing a lack of accountability, and political ridicule would result. After the case of *Ake* v. *Oklahoma* (470 U.S. 60 [1985]), indigent defendants were given a right to competent forensic evaluation by a psychiatrist. The workup includes basic history and medical, school, and job records. In current standards, the evaluator asks if the defendant rationally perceived reality, predicted natural consequences, and intended to kill at the time of the act. The insanity defense presumes "crazy" reasons for action and no understanding of moral significance.

Question-and-Answer Session
An audience member asked if new material is used for mitigation before sentencing. Dr. Poythress said many things are recognized in Florida as nonstatutory mitigators, such as military history, a broken family, and other historical and educational information.

Hickock and Smith both had organic brain damage and head injuries, which would have been entered into the record, and hanging would now be unlikely. Mr. Sevilla added that within a year, their convictions would have been opposed. All prospective jurors who opposed capital punishment also had been rejected from the jury. Under habeas corpus today, a confession that incriminates another defendant cannot be entered; this would be another reason to overturn the verdict. Had the defendants received better representation, they would have had a retrial. Mr. McCann added that, in conscience, he did not think he could have pursued the death penalty in this case.

Panel XVI. Concluding Remarks

Greg Klein, creative producer, "America's Most Wanted," Chevy Chase, Maryland, spoke about how this true-crime series has made 200 dramatic reenactments of crime situations and has a "capture rate" of 28 percent. Stories come from direct law enforcement contacts, the show's Web site, letters, or other TV personnel. The program receives amazing national coverage. Dramatic reenactments give the public a view of the criminal and small details about "why they are as they are." The small quirks in their personalities often "trip them up," resulting in capture. As an example, Mr. Klein told of a murder case involving a man who would hunt for his keys for 20 minutes each night. An observer called in about a person with this same peculiarity, who turned out to be the fugitive. Today, with publicity from a program such as "America's Most Wanted," Smith and Hickock probably would not have been able to stay on the run for 6 weeks.

Mr. Klein displayed selected film clips about major solved crime cases portrayed in the series. Ordinary people in their homes are given the opportunity to be "armchair detectives," help investigations, and contribute to the capture of "a myriad" of criminals.

Question-and-Answer Session
A participant asked if prosecutors request letters and information from the show. Mr. Klein said if the show has already aired, the request would be honored; prior to broadcast, however, the interviews or phone discussions are private, not public, record. The program is diligent about both presentation and preservation of privacy.

Another attendee asked whether shows were produced without the cooperation of victims' families. Mr. Klein said family members usually offer the story and their own insight. Occasionally, a family member does not want something shown, and the show honors the request. A person asked whether a fugitive had ever contacted them. Yes, said Mr. Klein, because he was upset about the clothing and inadequate good looks of the actor, not the criminal acts. The show often works with the local police, he said, and can benefit local crime prevention and public awareness.

Another attendee asked whether the producers were concerned that a similar looking innocent person may mistakenly be arrested. Mr. Klein said he does not think this happens often. The positive benefits outweigh the negative and may be considered "worth the inconvenience." In any marketplace, many lookalikes can be found, as he has observed from the casting process.

An attendee asked if the program had much success with cases of missing children. Mr. Klein said he wished the show's success rate were better. The show has profiled about 100 missing children, but only 12 have been brought home. A participant asked if there were similar programs in other countries. Mr. Klein said he knew of three: "UK Crime Watch," "India's Most Wanted," and a French version of the production.

www.ingramcontent.com/pod-product-compliance
Lightning Source LLC
Chambersburg PA
CBHW082240220526
45479CB00005B/1286